"Albert's Journey Footprints of An Immigrant is an uplifting story that provides you with an American hero. The challenges Albert faced and overcame were truly remarkable. You will meet a loving man who displayed dignity and strength, warmth and humor in the face of many demanding and unimaginable situations. Be prepared to cheerlead Albert throughout the read. Dolores A. Kelly Ed. D has written a touching story resonating to the strings of her heart. The songs she sings of her uncle, serenade you with faith, hope, courage and love. This book is an invitation to such beautiful music."

Loretta Lombardi
Pennsylvania
Middle School teacher

"An easy read for young teens to adults about a determined young immigrant, Albert to build a new life in America. Overcoming many hardships, he finds friends, builds a family and loves the life he lives. An inspiring story for everyone!"

T. K. William
Atlantic City, NJ

"Easy Quick Read. Ideal for the preteen to help realize the American Dream is possible no matter what kind of a childhood you are born into. Hard work, honesty, character and determination result in a successful life."

Sara Lee
California

Albert's Journey

Footprints of an Immigrant

By

Dolores A. Kelly

Cold Pond Press
New Jersey

Dolores A. Kelly

Published by Cold Pond Press, LLC
P. O. Box 4753
Cherry Hill, NJ 08034-4753
dakelly@coldpondpress.com

Copyright ©2009
Dolores A. Kelly, Ed. D.
All rights reserved.

No part of this publication may be reproduced or transmitted in any form or by any means, electronic or mechanical, including photocopying, recording, or by any information storage and retrieval system, without the written permission of the Publisher, except where permitted by law. Although every precaution has been taken in the preparation of this book, the publisher and author assume no responsibility for errors or omissions. Neither is any liability assumed for damages resulting from the use of information contained herein.

Editing: Ron Kenner
Illustration: Brigitta Sabatini

Library of Congress Control Number: 2009905474

ISBN: 978-0-578-02281-9

Printed in the United States of America

Preface

This book is in remembrance of my Uncle Albert who was such a loving and caring person. He was born in a sleepy Italian town. He came to the United States during the great wave of immigration in the first decades of the 20th Century and eventually set out on his own path, moving to California and planting his own family roots.

By purchasing this book, a portion of the proceeds will be donated to the Alzheimer's Association in memory of Albert De Frank.

> To order additional copies of this book please visit
> **albertsjourney.com**

Dolores A. Kelly

Dedicated to my beloved

Aunt Dorothy
Cousins
Dee Dee & Dan

Albert's Journey

Acknowledgments

In the preparation of this book there were many sources of support. First, I must recognize the continuing inspiration and support from my beloved Aunt Dorothy De Frank for whom this book is dedicated, and her daughter Dee Dee Collins and son Dan De Frank who assisted me with information from their childhood years. Dick Mouldon was an honorable and faithful friend of Uncle Albert and I appreciate all of the information he shared with me regarding his dearest friend Albert and their unrelenting friendship.

Steve Zahner, a firefighter from the Long Beach Airport, Daugherty Field Fire Station who works at Fire Station No. 16 sent me as much information as possible during the course of my research. He answered many questions I had regarding my uncle who retired from the station in August 1976. Uncle Albert was an Engineer who drove and operated the crash trucks that were at the airport during that time. Members

Dolores A. Kelly

of the Long Beach Firemen's Museum included Herb Bromley, Mike Kenney, and Glen Goodrich, president of the Long Beach Fireman's Museum. Rick Franz also assisted me with my research. I would like to give a special thank you, too, Rick, for all of the efforts in locating pictures and information regarding my uncle during the course of this writing. Rosemary Jordan thank you for your assistance with the readings and Les Roka for the first edit, and a special thank you to Ron Kenner for your editing expertise.

Finally, thanks to my cousin, Rita De Frank Hepner who assisted me with the information regarding the family's voyage from Italy to America, and to my husband John who spent tireless hours searching out information on my ancestry.

Table of Contents

CHAPTER ONE
Provenance 1

CHAPTER TWO
Traveling to America 9

CHAPTER THREE
Riding the Rails 40

CHAPTER FOUR
Friends for Life 53

CHAPTER FIVE
Returning to School 62

CHAPTER SIX
After Graduation 73

CHAPTER SEVEN
Grown Up and Having A Family 83

CHAPTER EIGHT
Friends, Family, and Camping Trips 95

CHAPTER NINE
A Chosen Career 116

CHAPTER TEN
A Good Life 151

Epilogue 165

Appendix 166

References 188

Chapter One

Provenance

Sant' Omero, Italy, was once an area where prehistoric settlements existed. There is a legend that Sant' Omero was based on a mount by Charlemagne after the devastation of the stronghold of Carrufo, which today is known as Garrufo. In 1154, it was known as Norman Territory. In 1276 it came under the control of the noble House of Acquaviva, and in the 16th century the Alarcon y Mendoza family assumed control.

Sant' Omero lies in the province of Teramo, in the northernmost part of Abruzzo, at the border of the Ascoli-Piceno Province by the Adriatic Sea. Today this small town, with more than 5,000 inhabitants, raises on a well-defined elevation of land between the Salinello and Vibrata rivers. The map shows a close-up of the Teramo area as it is today.

Situated at the center of the Italian peninsula, in the northeast province of Abruzzi, the town,

Dolores A. Kelly

almost ten miles (16 kilometers) from the Adriatic coastline, is made up of three villages. Sant' Omero, Garrufo, and Poggio Morello. The Abruzzo Region is divided into four provinces. L'Aquila (the largest), Chieti, Teramo (the most populous) and Pescara (Abruzzo's main economic center). These are divided further into 305 municipalities with a total population of 1.3 million people. Once an agricultural center, today it is developing into a manufacturing center. The region, less than two hours away from Rome by car, is connected by a seven-mile (12 kilometers) motorway that crosses through the National Park of Gran Sasso (Big Rock).

Albert's Journey

The Province of Teramo's landscape offers great variety. Within a 25-mile area (40 kilometers) it extends from the Adriatic Sea to the hills rising to more than 6500 feet (2000 meters) of the highest imposing Apennine Peaks. From north to south the landscape is grooved and wrinkled from the seven valleys of the rivers Tronto, Vibrata, Salinello, Tordino, Vomano, Piomba, and Fino. Tronto and Fino, only part of the territory, are neighboring provinces of Ascoli Piceno and Pescara. More than one third of the Province of Teramo covers the National Park of Gran Sasso and Laga Mountains. This locale covers more than 150,000 acres in the three regions consisting of five provinces. Corno Grande reaches an altitude above 9500 feet (2912 meters) and is the highest peak of

Dolores A. Kelly

all the Apennine Range. The region has valleys, woods, and forests along with caves, lakes, and rivers. Numerous plants, unlimited chestnut trees, beech trees, and white fir intertwine and blanket the landscape. The animals are many, an abundant kingdom of herbivores, predators, and birds of prey.

The region's unique physical beauty has always been a captivating attraction. The towns are just large enough to provide all that one needs, with open markets supplying all types of foods and goods. A myriad of tiny villages are balanced on rocky crests, dominated by castles with storybook towers that offer the perfect countryside view. The Abbeys sit in reclusive grandeur on the hilltops, their fascinating history of centuries past waiting to be rediscovered within their walls. Mini piazzas lie within each town where people gather daily for conversation and local activity.

After the middle of the 19th Century, the building of railways signaled changes, not all good. During the 1860s, 1870s, and 1880s tracks were added, but the railway did not contribute to the development of Abruzzo. There was a project in the region during the mid 1870s to drain Lake Fucino, then an unhealthy area near Avezzano. But the territory was not drained, and the land was saturated. This was where malaria broke out, killing many people. Although the soil in this part of the land was ideal for agriculture, the government had denied drainage and improvements.

Taking up the challenge, Count Alessandro Torlonia invested 45 million lira (today, the country's currency is the Euro) in the project to drain the lake. After the project was completed in 1885, he divided the land into 497 parcels of 60 acres each. These parcels were distributed to farmers from Abruzzo and other regions, yet benefited only a limited number of families. And despite this, the economy of the area remained unchanged. The 19th Century ended on a down note, with unkind living conditions and little evidence that the communities would be ready for the promise of a new century.

Immigration began in the late 1870s. People

had little money and few skills, were illiterate, and often spoke with a dialect recognizable only in their hometown. However, the men, stubborn in their purpose, wanted a land that promised jobs and the ability to put food on the table. To feed themselves and their families, these men took on any work they could find.

The early 1900s ushered in great waves of immigration bringing nearly 500,000 people to the United States of America, Argentina, and Brazil. Yet, many stayed in the region, deciding to relocate once Lake Fucino was drained and the fishing villages grew eventually into seaside resorts.

My ancestors lived in this small town of Sant' Omero which rises along an elevation between

Salinello and the Vibrata rivers. This town, a little over nine miles (16 kilometers) from the Adriatic Coast and more than 15 miles (25 kilometers) from Teramo, rises 682 feet (208 meters) above sea level. Above is a picture of the countryside as it is today. This beautiful landscape weaves with different shades of green rolling hills – a scenic backdrop like nowhere else.

Chapter Two

Traveling to America

Raising a family in Sant' Omero in the early 1900s was difficult at best. Therefore, in 1914, Pasquale DeFrancesco, the head of the household who also was my grandfather, decided he would go to the United States of America to make life better for himself and his family. His picture is shown below.

Dolores A. Kelly

Pasquale claimed he knew someone who would sponsor him in the United States. Once that connection was established he was able to book passage, and eventually he arrived in the Port of Philadelphia, Pennsylvania. Above is the flyer that was used to lure people to Philadelphia.

When he arrived, his sponsor met him and they traveled to the small town of Coatesville, Pennsylvania — about 35 miles west of Philadelphia — where Pasquale obtained work. Unlike the constant buzz of Philadelphia's city

Albert's Journey

life, Coatesville was a quiet, rural community where people grew food in their own gardens.

Below is a registration card of Pasquale, 37, working as a fireman in the Worth Steel Company in Claymont, Delaware. Grandpop, as I always called him, worked very hard and later obtained a job on the Pennsylvania Railroad.

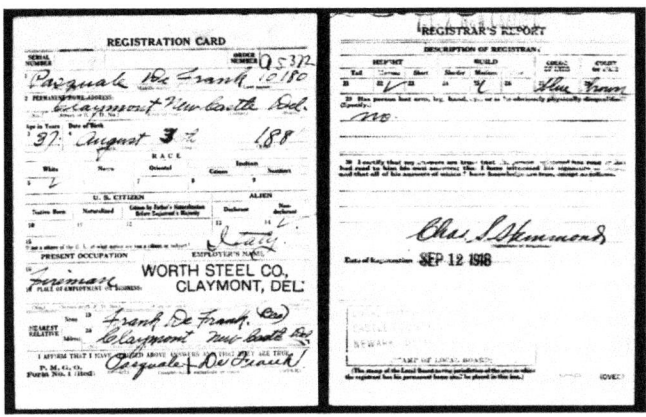

Working daily he was able to save enough money to send home to his wife and three children in Sant' Omero for their passage to America.

This is the story of Pasquale's youngest son, Albert and his dramatic, painful journey into the unknown to begin a new life in the United States of America. Once there, he would never return to his native land.

This is a land of rolling hills and green grasses, olive trees and grapevines. There are winding

Sant' Omero as it exists today in the Region of Abruzzo

roads and a kaleidoscope of landscapes. The mountains offer a refreshing sense of where we have been and where we are going. The flavor of the land with the aromas of foods cooking gives one a sense of warmth and feelings of home.

Yet, as beautiful as the landscape was and has always been, life in Italy was extraordinarily challenging in the early 20th century. Many Italians came to the United States, encouraged by the stories of others who said life was much better than in Sant' Omero.

On February 25, 1914 Albert was born. His father, introduced at the beginning of this chapter, was named Pasquale and his mother Camilla. The other members were Emidio Albert's brother, who was the oldest son, Santa, Albert's older sister, and Albert was the youngest. The other members of the DeFrancesco family who did not come to America have continued to live here in the house pictured below.

The home, in the family through the generations, will continue to be passed on to family members in the future.

The house has existed for many, many years and it is quite large. Deceiving from the outside, it appears ancient and dilapidated. Nevertheless, a side-glance proves otherwise. The two-story building is connected to another house and relatives of another part of the family live there. The rooms inside are spacious and decorated modestly. The second floor windows, with green shutters, are closed. The shutters on the first floor are large, stained hardwood. Designed to prevent the sun's rays from penetrating, these help to keep it cool inside during the summer months. They also cushion the traffic noise from the nearby road. The outside cement walls and stone trim frame a picture of antiquity. Every home in Italy has shutters to keep out the hot sun and the stone-and-concrete structure creates cooler temperatures inside the house. The balcony in the center of the house overlooks the street and passersby. Standing along the balcony is a statue of the Blessed Mother, the protector of the house and those who live inside, and those who have passed by chance. The house is located on the main road leading into the town center.

The house is so close to the road that it would be difficult to plant a garden. However, potted plants scattered near the front door make the entrance warm and inviting. Whenever relatives who lived in the United States went back to Sant'

Albert's Journey

Omero for vacation, there always was a warm, festive homecoming. However, Albert never made the trip back.

The entire family belonged to the local church of S. S. Annunziata in Sant' Omero where all the children were baptized, made their First Holy Communion, and received the Sacrament of Penance. The picture below shows the church as it still stands today.

S. S. Annunziata in Sant' Omero

The church is a pale salmon color with a side area in terra cotta. Along the street approaching the church are buildings in various colors of yellow, pink, tan and cream. The street is wide compared to most streets in Italy. On this particular day when the picture was taken there wasn't a cloud in the sky. It was an azure color with the sun shining bright while a few trees along the street provided shade from the hot sun.

This small, charming town is located in a rural area with rolling hills. Cool breezes from the not-so-far ocean act like a natural air conditioner. True to the town's warm and casual spirit, the people of Sant 'Omero are "salt of the earth" always helpful to those who ask for information. We must consider that almost all speak only Italian because it is far from a major city where English and other languages would be spoken. If you visit this area today, you might be tempted never to leave it because of its inviting charm, the great weather, and a casual, love-filled family lifestyle. This is a place where generations of old and young can easily communicate with each other.

Albert's lifetime adventure began when he was six. All children love adventure, but Albert knew that everything was about to change, going to a new land that wouldn't look anything like his home of Sant' Omero. Everyone was excited and yet anxiety touched each person in a special way. All three children were anxious about traveling, but the excitement and joy,

Albert's Journey

which surrounded him and his siblings, also was overwhelming. The entire family – Camilla, Emidio, Santa, Alberto, and Camilla's sister-in-law, Maria – was on the verge of changing their quiet, casual lives forever. Nevertheless, Camilla questioned what lied ahead. The children — Emidio, Santa and Alberto – asked so many questions of their mother who wondered, too, about what was going to happen.

Camilla DeFrancesco circa 1940s

Camilla, their mother, was anxious and concerned because she would be crossing the Atlantic with three small children. She thought about the sinking of the Titanic Ocean Liner on April 15, 1912 when the ship hit an iceberg and sank. A little over two hours later, it fell two miles below the surface. There were

1312 passengers and crew who lost their lives, and Camilla did not want to travel on a ship anywhere.

This didn't matter to Pasquale who was in America. He already had the tickets purchased beforehand and wanted Camilla here. However, she realized once she went she would never return to her homeland and her loved ones.

Camilla told the children to begin packing and they were excited laughing and thinking of this new venture. She insisted all the children say their good-byes to their aunts, uncles, cousins and friends. However, her thoughts were focused on this new and strange land even while she knew her husband would do everything to make the family happy. Pasquale had gone before her six years ago, and he was confident that everything would be fine once the family arrived and everybody would be happy together as a family.

Another reason she didn't want to come to this strange place, she would know no one other than her immediate family members, and life would be very lonely. She realized that she would have no friends until she was there for sometime, but also wanted to be with her husband. She packed everything she owned to set out for the new world. Still, she could not escape her reservations about making the trip. She hoped she had done the right thing in making the voyage and leaving her homeland.

Albert's Journey

The time had come and Albert's father sent for the family in 1921. He had accumulated enough money for everyone to make the voyage, but Albert's mother Camilla was still terrified to cross the Atlantic Ocean. Pasquale assured Camilla that the trip would be safe and they would be very happy in America. She was still reluctant about traveling but Pasquale gave her an ultimatum; she was not pleased, but decided to make the journey to the new world. All she could think about was how lonely it would be and that she would miss her family and friends.

Albert, his mother Camilla, and his brother Emidio, and sister Santa all departed from their family's home in Sant' Omero, Italy and took along Pasquale's sister Maria. They boarded the train to Naples, Italy in March 1921. After arriving in Naples, they then boarded the Anchor Line S. S. Italia at the port of Naples on March 18, 1921. A copy of the ticket showing that they traveled in third class is on page 22. The voyage took 17 days.

Since Pasquale had accumulated enough money for the voyage but they only had tickets to travel in third class, the most inexpensive way to travel on a passenger ship, there were no amenities and everyone was squeezed together. The voyage across the Atlantic Ocean appeared as though it would never end. However, they finally arrived on April 4, 1921, at Boston,

Dolores A. Kelly

Albert's Journey

Ticket for voyage

Massachusetts. The ship should have arrived in New York City, but something unknown occurred and it was diverted to Boston.

During the early 1900s, ships crossing the Atlantic Ocean took about two to three weeks. We can see from the photo shown on page 20-21 that the passenger manifest of alien passengers for the United States showed all the members of the family as well as Maria, Pasquale's sister, arriving together.

Albert's Journey

The passenger manifest stated the family name and given name of Camilla, Emidio, Santa, Alberto, and Pasquale's sister Maria.

After seven years, reuniting the family was important for Pasquale. He had come first to the United States to find work in 1914 because there was no work in his homeland of Italy. He sent money back to the family in Sant' Omero and decided that when he was settled here in America he would send for his wife and three children, and so he did. He wanted the family with him because he had missed them terribly and was very lonely. He also wanted to have everyone here before the spring ended so he could plant his garden and prepare to have all the food they needed for the winter and the following spring.

Because traveling in March was still winter the seas were rough and there were times they all felt that they would not make it to America. The temperature on the sea fluctuated from cold to very cold because of the winds and the dampness. The ship swayed back and forth and some passengers found it difficult to keep food

SS Italia

down. On board, Albert had been missing for sometime. His mother went into a panic and thought he might have fallen overboard because of the rough seas. Speaking in Italian, she alerted the passengers nearby and someone interpreted for her to the captain, who spoke English, to be on the lookout for Albert because he was so small. However, the crew and passengers looked urgently and eventually he was found nestled under one of the lifeboats, afraid, wondering when they would reach the new land of America. Emidio and Santa thought they would not make it to their new home because of seasickness. They felt weak because they couldn't keep any food down. All of the children were restless and sick from the constant wave motions of the sea. The sea finally became calm once again, but the air was still cold and the weather always cool, damp, and dreary. When they were supposed to arrive in the port of New York, problems arose with the ship. Even today, no one knows what caused a change in ports but the ship finally docked in the Boston harbor.

When they reached their destination, Camilla had to show the customs and immigration officers her passport along with identification of the three children, their ages and sex. Below is a copy of what her passport looked like in 1921.

When they disembarked at Boston, the boys noted that other young boys were wearing different types of pants. Camilla told Emidio and Alberto the pants were knickers. During the 1920s, the boys in America wore knickers that

went just below the knee and were always worn with long stockings. Albert's mother decided that when they came to America she would make the boys wear long pants. When they arrived in the new world, Emidio said, "The Italians brought the style of long pants to America!"

Finally, the long voyage was over. They had come to America, but this was Boston – not New York. They needed to find passage on a train to meet Pasquale in Coatesville, Pennsylvania. He found a house there to make a permanent home in the new country. Camilla was unable to speak English and relied on others to ask how she and her children and sister-in-law would get to this small town to meet her husband. Thanks to the enthusiastic help of others who spoke Italian, she was directed to the train station and the train master showed her the schedule and the train she and the others would need to take to board the proper train to reach her destination of Coatesville, Pennsylvania.

The next picture shows the Coatesville Train Station that was built in 1865 and was very popular at the time. It was and still is located at Third Avenue and Fleetwood Streets. The building was originally a three story building with two wings. The first and third stories were used as habitation and entirely divided from the second story which was used for railroad functions. People who lived in this rural area

Albert's Journey

would be able to travel easily to and from the city of Philadelphia. This was the only major means of transportation, especially for the immigrants, who now were arriving daily in this small community.

Pennsylvania Railroad Station, Coatesville, PA

From the *Coatesville Weekly Times* on April 10, 1886: *"The Pennsylvania Railroad Company, which is ever looking to the comfort of its partrons, has placed a lamp, which is kept burning all night at the station in this Borough. It is a great accommodation, not only to the partrons of the road, but to the public in general, and for which they deserve the thanks of the traveling community."*

The family settled in a house at the top of a hill. The house, larger than the one they'd occupied in Sant' Omero, had a foyer, living room, dining room, kitchen, an enclosed porch, three bedrooms, one bath, and an attic that could be used for storage or another bedroom. The basement could be used to make wine and provide storage for the entire year along with all the fruits and vegetables they would harvest from the garden. Camilla knew how to jar fruits and vegetables so they could enjoy the fresh taste of produce throughout the upcoming winter months.

The house had an enclosed porch at the rear. This was where the family entered, so the front foyer would not be dirty. The back part of the house was where Camilla did the wash and ironed the clothes. When she baked and canned fruits and vegetables, she used this part of the house to prepare and store the warm jars until they cooled. They were then stored in the cool, dark basement so they could be used during the winter months. Next to the house was a very large lot, almost an acre, where Pasquale and Camilla, along with Emidio and Santa, planted a massive garden so they would eat well during all the seasons. There were fruit trees of apples, sickle pears, peaches, and many vegetables. There also was lettuce, corn, carrots, fennel, potatoes, beans, peas, onions, tomatoes, cantaloupes, peppers, cucumbers, corn, eggplant, and zucchini as well as fruits including watermelon, strawberries, raspberries, and grapes perfect for homemade wine and preserves. They planted herbs such as basil, Italian flat leaf parsley, mint, oregano, sage, garlic, and many colorful flowers. The outer shed above the garden held the tools for the garden. Chickens were raised for eggs and meat for the Sunday meal. The following picture shows part of the large garden that provided constant nourishment for the family's daily life. Pictured on the next page from left to right, are Albert (L) Emidio (center) and Pasquale, the father (R).

The garden had many beautiful flowers, which attracted bees for pollination. They needed to purchase very little for food except flour to make bread for their daily meals, sugar for sweetener, and coffee for the adult beverage.

Dolores A. Kelly

Albert's mother made everything from scratch. There were no fast foods in the 1920s. All children ate what their mother prepared for them. Everything was homemade from soups, sauces and stews to desserts for daily treats. All foods were prepared from the garden and set for the evening meal.

Following is another picture of the garden and the grandchildren gathered for a picture. (The grandchildren from left to right, Dan, Dee, Dolly, Mary, Rita, Jimmy, and me Dolores in Jimmy's arms). The garden provided plenty and was enjoyable, especially on Sundays, because that was the time for family and everyone ate together.

One of Albert's duties was to go down into the basement, which the family called the

cellar, and to pick the sprouts off the potatoes. The potatoes were harvested from the garden and stored in the cellar along with everything else that would be eaten during the winter. Albert had plenty of other jobs around the house. He tended the garden with his older brother Emidio and sister Santa, picking stones out of the soil, hoeing, and watering. Everyone had specific chores. Santa's job was to take the husks off the corn along with the silk threads that stuck to the kernels. Emidio did whatever needed to be done. He painted the house, whitewashed the basement, painted the porch, put the screens up on the windows for summer to keep the flies and mosquitoes out, and helped cultivate the grounds for the garden so they could be fruitful. Everyone's job was important; otherwise, the winter would be a lean, difficult period for food.

Then a newcomer arrived in the family but stayed for only a short time. Sadly, Antonio did not live very long because of health reasons, and passed away quite young. Little is known about Antonio and he was never spoken about as time passed. A few years after the family arrived in the United States another child was born – a girl named Maria, who was my mother. She was the baby of the family and I am sure she was loved very much. As she was growing up, she became very close to Albert, her beloved brother. The picture below shows Maria Rose with her mother and father circa 1923-1925.

Albert's Journey

Soon after the birth of Maria, the Census was taken. Sometimes in America people had difficulty pronouncing and spelling the Italian names. At that time the family name was changed from DeFrancesco to DeFrank. Therefore, with the passing of time and the children growing older, their last name was changed so that people in America would be able to pronounce their name without difficulty. Immigrants coming to America eagerly wanted to be Americanized. Most would try not to speak their native tongue and would only speak English. They thought this was the best thing for their children. However, many children grew up learning English, forgetting or not ever knowing their native language.

The children were growing older and their responsibilities increased. They all tried to find odd jobs to bring home money to help with the family. But the Great Depression that started in 1929 made it that much more difficult to find odd jobs that normally would have gone to young boys and girls but were now being desperately taken by adults who had lost their regular jobs.

Emidio and Albert shoveled snow and coal for the neighbors as well as for the local businessmen. Albert, a friendly fellow, tried to get people to hire him for any out-of-the-ordinary job available. He had a dynamic personality and made many friends while growing up in this ethnic neighborhood. Everyone spoke the same language, Italian sprinkled with little English, and they all went to school together. Parents wanted their children to speak English but children tended to feel more comfortable with their native tongue.

His friends knew Albert as Al: a kind and gentle human being with a low-keyed voice, great disposition, dynamic personality, and mild manner. He tried as hard as he could to make extra money, but his father never believed him when he was out late shoveling snow or coal for the neighbors. He had an unhappy childhood in the late 1920s as he was approaching his teenage years. His father constantly hit and yelled at him and the abuse was very difficult for Albert to handle, so he decided that he had enough of being whipped by his father. His father would strike him for everything he did. Albert reached the stage where he could not stand it any longer. He didn't want to fight back, because his father would continue to hit him. He even punched him and beat him with a hose. He tied him to a post in the cellar and continued to beat Albert brutally. One day when he went to school, Albert said to himself that he just could never go home and face the brutality again. His father abused him so much that he decided to run away. He didn't know exactly what day he would leave, or where he was going, but it would be soon.

Uncle Chescino, Pasquale's brother and Albert's uncle, was educated in Italy and came to America before Pasquale. He was an engineer and worked for Bethlehem Steel in western Pennsylvania. He visited the family quite often with his wife Grace, and before they returned home he presented each child with a gold coin. However, after Uncle Chescino left, Pasquale would take all the coins from the children. The children were truly saddened and disappointed when this happened. Albert became infuriated with what his father had done and thought that it was unfair to do this. Because Uncle Chescino and Aunt Grace didn't have any children, they treated all of their nieces and nephews as if they were their own.

Albert's father had always made wine. But these were Prohibition days. In fact, the chief of police was Pasquale's best customer. One day the chief told Pasquale the government's revenue agents were going to raid his house the next day. Albert's father had the children take all the wine out of the barrels and fill everything they could find to put wine in. They hid the wine and filled the barrels with water. Then the revenue agents came and emptied all the barrels out, only to discover it was all

Dolores A. Kelly

water. Pasquale was a coy and clever man. He wouldn't allow anyone to interfere with his work and family. Absolutely no one would take anything from him.

Another event occurred on Albert's way home from school one day. Albert was always looking for work, and one time, the rabbi stopped him and said, "Albert, would you shovel the snow off of the steps?" Albert said, "Yes, because I would like to make some money." So he shoveled the snow from the steps and when he was finished the rabbi gave him a dime. This frustrated Albert. He'd worked so hard and only made a dime, but it still was a dime and he put it in his pocket. However, by the time he got home, about 4:30 p.m., it already was dark, like any day in a Pennsylvania winter.

His father said, "Why are you late coming home, you worried your mother." He ordered Albert to go down into the cellar. Albert knew he was in for a beating and when his father came down he beat Albert with his belt once again and took the dime away from him that he had earned from shoveling snow. For Albert, a teenager now, this was the last straw. He knew he had to get away from this brutality. He was so abused that he felt he could not physically handle it anymore. He was only 16 and in the tenth grade, but he had become so miserable over what his father constantly did to him.

Albert's Journey

The neighbors knew how his father treated him, but no one would say anything about the abuse. They didn't want to say anything against the father because he seemed a good neighbor.

This made Albert's decision very easy. His emotions were mixed because he was sad to leave his family, whom he loved very much, but he also wanted a better life with no abuse. Thus he knew that he needed to run away and start anew. Albert, deciding that life had to be better the farther away from home he could travel. He wanted to find a place where he could be content and create a new life for himself. Well he found it and this is his story.

During the early part of the 20th Century it was common for children to run away from home, and just as dangerous as it is today. One day on the way to school Albert said, "I'm leaving for the west," and was determined to travel westward, but the only way he could do this was to take the train. He had no money and thought that the only way out was to try to leap onto a train. Albert was now 16 and in the tenth grade. He thought about this for a long time and on his way to school one morning he decided this would be his opportunity to leave home and never return. He knew he would miss his brother and sisters, but wanted a better life and this was the only way to have it.

He went to school in the morning and thought

about nothing except leaving home. While he was sitting in the classroom he was determined that this is what he must do. He needed to leave quickly. He was in the local public school on Main Street, in class, and decided this was the best time to do it. He grabbed a classmate's umbrella and jumped out the second story window, thinking that the umbrella would help his fall. However, the umbrella turned inside out and he fell on his bottom. He then ran to the train station and hopped into a boxcar on a freight train traveling westward.

Chapter Three

Riding the Rails

Wow! What an electrifying trip! Going from town to town Albert was so happy to see different people and inspiring places. He felt bad that he had to leave his baby sister, Maria, whom he called Mary, but he felt this was the best thing to do and start a new life. As he passed through every town on the train it was an adventure. Some towns had tall buildings and others not so tall structures, but each town had its own set of memorable sights. Oh! How Albert enjoyed telling his story.

He met many people on the freight trains going west. At that time one might have called him a hobo. He stayed along the train tracks with others who were hopping trains to go to a place where life was better but with no specific town in mind. Albert would disembark the train to find work and food. One day while walking down a dirt country road in Indiana he noticed watermelon vines on both sides of the road.

He loved watermelons. His father grew them in the garden and he ate them every summer. Watermelons were lying about and there was one on the side of the road. Albert was very hungry, so he stopped, and picked up the watermelon and when he did a shotgun went off. He looked up and saw a farmer coming toward him, dressed in bib coveralls and carrying a shotgun that he pointed straight at Albert. He dropped the watermelon and ran as fast as he could. Albert said, "From that day on I swore I would never – ever – take anything that didn't belong to me." He ran so fast from the farmer that he recalled it wasn't the first time he had to outrun the bullets.

Riding freight trains occasionally made for a risky guessing game. He would jump on to a train and hide in a boxcar, and any train that was moving that he could get on, he would take. He never knew where the train was going. He would find out where he was when he got off at the end of the line. When the train would start to slow down he would try to jump off before it went into the train yard. If he couldn't jump off ahead of time, once in the train yard, the yard police would be there with rifles. They would shoot at him and whoever was traveling with him. So Albert learned to run fast. He said, "I had to outrun those bullets every time I got off a train in a train yard."

During his travels he would find a farmhouse and go to the back door, knock on the door, and ask if he could work for food. He said, "I was always hungry." Nine times out of ten the farmer's wife would have a job for him such as chopping wood or picking crops and he would eat pretty well. Some people offered to let him sleep in an outbuilding, a barn or a porch. He remembered how fortunate he had been that everyone was so good to him. They would allow him to wash up with the hose or a little washtub. Many times the farmers would give him clean socks or clean underwear. He always managed. The only thing he ever attempted to steal was that one watermelon because he was so hungry. He swore he would never steal again.

Albert zigzagged all the way across the United States. He loved the sites he saw in the country. It took him many weeks to reach his final destination. Meanwhile, he met an older man who was going to Yellowstone National Park to fight a forest fire. The man talked about how the fire was destroying the park and how well it paid to help put out the blaze. Albert asked the man if he could travel along with him, and they rode freight trains and thumbed for rides. However, by the time they arrived at Yellowstone Park, the fire was out. Albert left his newfound friend and went on his way alone. Later he heard of another fire in National Yosemite Park, California. He met another man traveling with him in the boxcar – this time, much older than Albert – who was going to Yosemite Park to fight the fires. He told Albert that the pay was very good, too. Albert asked if he could travel with the man and try to make some money. Because he was penniless he felt this was a good way to make a few dollars. As the men approached Yosemite Park they discovered that the fires were out. The man that Albert was traveling with decided to head for the California Coast and Albert asked the man if he could tag along. He traveled along for a while, and then decided to separate somewhere out in the desert.

Albert was in the desert alone and tired of walking. He started to thumb for rides, and ended up wherever it would take him. Albert had not planned on any specific town or state. He wanted to go west to start his new life, and to be as far away as possible from his abusive father. He would go with anyone who would give him a ride.

In 1931 Albert came into the town of Long Beach. The climate was warm and sunny, which was in his favor, because he had no place to stay. What a site to see! Gee, he thought, the trees looked different. They were tall and had narrow trunks and palms at the top. He said that as soon as he saw the Pacific Ocean and beach, he immediately fell in love with them. This new place would be his home.

Now he wanted to discover all the different things in California. This was such a beautiful unusual place. In Southern California Albert noticed that the air was warm and everyone seemed very relaxed. He wanted to experience everything that was new to him. Because it was still warm he noticed the color of the hills were light brown, really unusual for him because he was accustomed to seeing plenty of green during the warm season. He learned that the low amount of rainfall provided the landscape with this tan color because it was very dry. However, during the winter months, there was ample rainfall and everything turned green once again.

He decided he needed to sleep somewhere but he had no money, and ended up sleeping on the beach under the Rainbow Pier, in the sand. He just loved the beach so much he never wanted to leave the area.

Albert's Journey

Albert slept under the pier in the sand

Albert slept on the beach for sometime, but he needed to work so he could eat and find his own place to live. So he set out to the local bowling alley to set up pins. The bowling alleys were not automated then. Pin boys at the other end of the alleys would set the pins at the end of each frame for the next player. This way he would make change and buy food. Albert struggled a great deal, but he didn't give up. He also collected glass milk bottles and turned them in for a penny apiece. He worked on the Long Beach Pike that was the center of entertainment in the Long Beach area. It was an amusement park that was all cement, and it was a great part of the city's history. Located on the waterfront, it featured the roller coaster, the Wooden Cyclone Racer, that ran from the 1930s to the 1960s. It had a merry-go-round, an arcade, a hand-carved carousel, the Municipal Auditorium and all sorts of games. In addition to the rides, games, and a bowling alley, there were snow cones and salt-water taffy. Because the Pike was on the water and featured all of these attractions one hundred years ago, it was known as the West Coast's Coney Island.

There was also the Plunge, a salt-water swimming pool for those who did not want to swim in the Pacific Ocean. Children also knew this area as an amusement zone. At one concession stand, beachgoers could throw balls at wooden milk bottles for prizes. Albert worked setting up the milk bottles continuously so he could make money to buy food. He was always hungry and felt like he never had enough to eat. He was still a growing boy, soon to become a man. He would do anything to make money for

Scene on the Pike, Long Beach, California

Albert's Journey

View from Rainbow Pier, Long Beach, California

food, and this was the only way he survived.

Albert loved the ocean. The Rainbow Pier was beautiful and Albert would swim in the pier area where they had the boat dock. There was a float out in the middle of the lagoon, and the manager of the area rented putt-putt boats. A putt-putt boat, with a small engine, dates back to the 19th century. Albert soon became acquainted with Johnny White who owned the business.

Albert persisted in asking Johnny for a job, but "there was no job," Johnny insisted. However, Johnny said, "I'll bring you a cot from home and you could be my night watchman." This way Albert could sleep on the cot out on the float where the putt-putt boats were tied up. Finally, Albert had a place to sleep inside of a little shack on the float that was made of old wood and splintery with white paint. He was relieved at last that he had a place to stay and was out of the elements at night.

He had a roof over his head for about two years, sleeping on the boat float. He would still find odd jobs to make change to keep himself going. Everyday all he could think of and say to himself was, "What am I going to do today to make enough money in order to buy food?" Albert was preoccupied each day, wondering what he would do that day to earn money. At this point, he had become very thin from not eating regularly. There was a restaurant three blocks from the Pike and one day Albert asked Mr. Hopi who owned the restaurant if he could work for food. Mr. Hopi said, "You could wash the pots and pans, and then I'll give you

Boat float with shack and Putt-Putt Boats, was Albert's new home

Albert's Journey

something to eat." Albert now became the dishwasher, washing the dishes, pots and pans. Mr. Hopi permitted Albert to go and help himself to anything he wanted to eat. He thought that this was just extraordinary. He was so happy to have one square meal a day. Mr. Hopi also told Albert that, "Anytime you want something to eat, you come by and I will have a job here for you washing dishes and the pans."

Therefore, Albert went back, day after day and washed the dishes, pots, and pans. Then he decided to volunteer to mop the floor in the restaurant. The Hopi's were very happy to have Albert work for them. He worked very hard and was dependable, and Albert was especially happy to eat one regular meal a day. He was also happy to be away from his father's abuse. Everyone he met was nice to him in this new town. He liked it here so much he decided this was where he would stay. Albert, at last, found a peaceful home.

Albert had a passionate enthusiasm for the ocean, enjoyed the beach, and could stay in the ocean all day long. He loved to swim and became a beautiful diver. He learned to dive off the deck of the boat float and out in the lagoon on a lifeguard float. He never had any diving lessons but he taught himself to dive with grace. Because of this he decided he wanted to be a lifeguard. Al needed a steady job, and he enjoyed the ocean and wanted to be helpful to those who needed him. One of Albert's buddies told him that he was going to go to Oregon to see about getting a job working on the Grand Coolie Dam, and he wanted to know if Albert would like to go along with him. Well, he decided to go. They hitchhiked up to Oregon and they did get work on the dam. They both did concrete work and when that job ran out they hitchhiked back to Long Beach, California. When he returned to Long Beach Albert decided to be a lifeguard.

Since Albert wanted to be a lifeguard he had to go through a rigorous training program. He spent many days on the beach learning the "how of the operation" and the many techniques lifeguards learn to be effective and efficient. The picture below shows Albert as a lifeguard; once

The beach Albert loved.
He wanted to be a lifeguard here.

he had mastered the program he began making a weekly salary for himself.

Albert worked on the beach every day and was the night watchman in the old splintery boat shack at night.

He began making friends every day. His first friend was Johnny White. Albert's friendly personality made him very popular as a lifeguard. It was as a lifeguard that he would meet his lifelong friend to be – Harold King.

Albert holding buoy in front of the paddleboard

Chapter Four

Friends for Life

The picture below is of Albert and Harold working as lifeguards along the beach in Long Beach, California. It was truly unbelievable the way he met Harold. Albert was a small framed and underfed man, but very strong.

Albert and Harold life guarding at the beach

Harold came walking down the beach one day. He was very muscular and well built and was quite a figure of a man compared to Albert. Albert sized him up and approached him and said, "You really think you're tough, don't' you?" Harold responded, "No, I don't think I'm tough." Albert kept taunting him, and said, "You look tough and you think you're tough, and you're not as tough as you look, and I could beat you up." Harold said, "No, you can't." Albert said, "Yes, I can." They both squabbled back and forth. A shoving match ensued and this went on for quite some time. A crowd started to gather and they finally got each other in a headlock.

Harold would say, "Do you give up?" Albert would say, "No, do you give up?"

Neither one wanted to give up as the crowd edged them on and they continued to throw punches. Harold then said, "Look, my mother expects me to come home for dinner and I'm late, now if you let go, I'll let go." Harold asked Albert if he would like to come home and have dinner with his family, and Albert said, "I'd love it!" They let go and from that minute on they were best friends for the rest of their lives. The two amazed each other as time passed because they both enjoyed the same things, especially their love of the beach and the Pacific Ocean, along with diving into the water.

Harold and Albert decided to create a diving

Albert's Journey

act. A large hotel in Palm Springs, California was asking for water acts. Harold and Albert decided they could make some money so they put on a beautiful diving show for the customers at the hotel pool. They dived all day and made five dollars for the show.

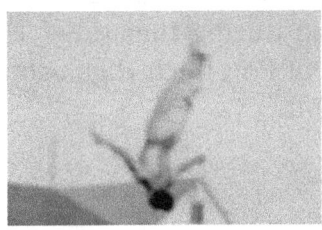

During the early 1930s, Harold was going to high school in Long Beach. Albert kept thinking, oh, I would give anything to go back to school and get my diploma. However, Albert had to stay at the beach even though it was time for the guys and gals to return to the classroom. September came and everyone started school and they weren't on the beach anymore so Albert was left alone on the beach and the boat float. He was lonely and decided that he needed an education and wanted to learn as much as he could so he could make something of himself. He read whatever papers he found and wanted to be informed about everything.

Albert had the idea of getting back into school and went up to Poly Tech High School in Long

Beach and tried to enroll himself. The school had quite a history. It was founded in 1895 but there was a massive earthquake in 1933 that almost destroyed the building. The devastation was tremendous. The high school had many walls and ceilings that collapsed and as the picture below shows it was just unreal what the school went through during that time. The following pictures are of Poly Tech High School when the earthquake hit.

Long Beach, California, Earthquake March 10, 1933, killed 120 people, with hundreds of people injured and about $40 million (a substantial amount at that time) in damages. The epicenter was located just offshore near Newport Beach. The earthquake with a magnitude of 6.3 occurred at 5:54 p.m. Main entrance of Polytechnic High School in Long Beach. Note wreckage in entrance. Photo from H.M. Engle (eng00007).

Long Beach Polytechnic High School. March 19, 1933. Photo courtesy of W. L. Huber.

The damages by this earthquake at Long Beach and the surrounding areas were extensive. It was written in the newspapers that most of the damage happened to buildings that were unreinforced masonry and this affected many of the schools. There were 120 people in the area that died in the earthquake. This photo is yet another snapshot of the extensive damage to Poly Technic High School in Long Beach.

Earthquakes kept occurring but they didn't bother Albert. He loved it here and considered it home. Albert kept returning to the school because he wanted an education to help himself have a better life. Even though there was damage to the school Albert still wanted to get that education, which meant so much to him. He knew what he needed and was determined to return to school no matter what it took. The administrators at the school kept rejecting Albert and his heart was broken. He went in several times and just said, "I really want to go to school. Please let me get enrolled and go to school?" The administrator said, "No, you don't have an address, or a guardian so we can't let you go to school." They turned him down again and again. Summer vacation ended and, once again, Albert was alone on the boat float, and doing odd jobs to survive while others were in school.

A year passed and Albert became very friendly with Mrs. Hunter, a terrific woman and the pie baker in the Hopi Restaurant where Albert still washed dishes. He continued to work for the

Albert's Journey

Hopi's because this was the only way he could have that one great meal a day. He told Mrs. Hunter he wanted to go to school and mentioned what the school administration said about going back to school. She told Albert that if he needed an address he could sleep on her front porch using a cot she had stored away. He thought this was great. It was close to the restaurant so he still washed dishes and mopped the floor and was able to secure his meals in exchange for his work.

However, he did not have any parents or a guardian to sign papers to enroll him in school. Mrs. Hunter said, "I'll be your guardian." Albert and Mrs. Hunter went up to the main office at school to enroll him in high school to complete his education. The principal advised both Mrs. Hunter and Albert that there was a proper way to do this and Albert had to have formal papers sent back to his parents in the east, allowing Mrs. Hunter to be his guardian. The signed papers were to allow Albert to show that Mrs. Hunter would be responsible for his education, and this allowed him to be enrolled in high school to complete his education. This was the only way Albert was able to go back to high school. He would do anything to have the proper education, be a high school graduate, and have his diploma.

Finally, Albert would be going to Poly Tech

Dolores A. Kelly

High School in Long Beach, California. Below is a picture of the high school after the earthquake and restoration of the school was underway.

*The Long Beach Polytechnic High School Auditorium.
There were only a few vertical and horizontal
cracks in back in the scene room.
Photo courtesy of H. M. Engle.*

CHAPTER FIVE

Returning to School

Poly Tech High School requested records from the school Albert had attended in the east. At that time the mail was very slow in coming. Because of the delay in confirming his status, the school placed Albert into the ninth grade. This put Albert one year behind because his records were so slow in getting there from Pennsylvania. He did quite well, and put all of his energy into his studies. When the school records finally arrived and were reviewed, the administration felt he was doing so well that they would place him in the tenth grade where he belonged. If it weren't for Mrs. Hunter giving Albert a place to sleep on her front porch and a home address as well as being his guardian, he would have never had been able to return to school and obtain his high school diploma. Education was very important to Albert. He knew that if he did not return to school and graduate that life would be miserable for him

Albert's Journey

and he would not be able to provide for himself or a family in the future.

Albert then decided that he needed to find another job. He looked around a bit and found a job delivering newspapers in the morning before school. No matter the circumstances, Albert always found a way to make a dollar and support himself.

Since he went back to school, Albert and Harold continued their friendship. They both were interested in the trampoline and tumbling and became very good tumblers. They built their own very large trampoline net and they became so good they put an act together and would demonstrate their skills in gymnastics. They raised money for different events in Long Beach and continued to put on shows. The crowds loved them.

When a circus came to town and saw their act, they immediately wanted to hire both of

them, but Harold would not go with the circus. Albert really wanted to go because he felt this would be his best possible way to have a weekly salary, but because Albert was Harold's best friend Albert stayed behind and forgot about the circus, too. Albert never wanted to part from his best friend Harold.

While Albert was in high school he took cooking classes to get something to eat. He always wanted to be in a position to satisfy his hunger pangs. He enjoyed cooking classes and always ate all the food. His teacher thought that he just might be the next great chef of their time. He also became involved with sports and decided to be on the football team.

When Albert was a sophomore he was able to join Poly Tech's junior varsity football team. His coach was Charley Church. In 1934 the junior varsity team was composed entirely of sophomores. That year, as written in the 1935 school yearbook, the squad "completed a successful season considering the odds, which they were up against."

The 1934 yearbook "Caerulea" shows the junior varsity football team of Poly Tech, with Albert in the first row, last person on the right. The team members developed a strong friendship in the field of sports. Most students would be seniors the following year and these young men, the administration felt, would display leadership and be the ideal role models for the younger students.

The Poly Tech's junior varsity team was matched against the varsity teams of schools with smaller enrollments. In 1934 the sophomores did extraordinarily well to nab one win out of the games played. The lack of experience on the part of the junior varsity and an incapability to generate an adequate defense were the two characteristics which hindered the junior varsity team throughout the season. According to Poly Tech's Caerulea 1934 yearbook, they opened their season against a dominant Tustin team which defeated Poly 32-6. Poly's team was unable to handle the aggressive power thrust hurled against them by the more experienced squad. This was the difference between a victory and defeat for the Poly junior varsity team. Even though Albert's team was unable to get a winning season, he made every effort to be the best he could be for his fellow teammates. See how the 1935 yearbook summarized the JV team's season and note the editor's writing style widely popular for yearbooks at the time:

Pitted against the varsities of schools with smaller enrollments than their own, the sophomores did exceptionally well to garner one victory out of five games played. Lack of experience and inability to produce an airtight defense were the two characteristics, which hampered the sophomores throughout the season.

Opening their season against a powerful Tustin eleven, the Poly fledglings were decisively defeated 32-6. Being unable to cope with the offensive powers thrust at them by the more experienced squad was the difference between victory and defeat for the sophomores. In their second clash of the season, the Jackrabbits encountered Narbonne High and were again defeated, this time 26-6.

Hitting their stride in the next game, Poly's junior varsity handed Garden Grove's varsity a 19-7 setback for the first win of the year. Displaying an improved brand of football all the way, the Jackrabbits took the lead early and held it throughout the tussle. In their next game, the junior varsity suffered a severe let down and were defeated 26-0 by Banning's varsity aggregation.

Winding up their season with their annual

Albert's Journey

intra city battle with Woodrow Wilson, the Jackrabbits journeyed to Stephens Field, only to be turned back by a 6-0 score. Outstanding players were Irwin and Hawks, guards: Baird, tackle: Sexton, end; Wilcox and DeFrank, halfbacks; and Howard, fullback.

At the beginning of his junior year – the 1934-1935 school year – Albert made the varsity football team. Given his experience on the junior varsity team he'd learned all of the executions and behaviors from previous games, which made him more astute to execute the proper plays.

Albert front and center on the varsity football team During the 1934-1935 school year Albert and all the other juniors had an opportunity to cultivate their interest and pride in school activities. Albert had developed in the field of sport, and football was his passion. The 1935 yearbook "Caerulea" noted that when the students became seniors it was "confidently predicted that they would display a marked leadership," and they would "be worthy of the emulation always accorded seniors by the lower classmen."

He was on the "A" Football Team and his captain was E. Howard. Albert felt exhilarated playing football, maintaining a healthy physique and a sharp mind, as he worked hard in school, studied, and played sports. He also enjoyed the camaraderie of the other players throughout the school year.

Being a junior, Albert was so proud to make the varsity team. He was 20 years old. Because he had to wait so long to return to school he was three to four years older than his classmates in the 11th grade. The age gap did not matter to him. He knew he was learning a great deal and would graduate the following year. His thoughts were focused on the future, so he needed to make good grades, graduate high school and find a decent job and earn enough money. Then there would be a future for him, much better than he had in the east and eventually a good home life down the road.

As a junior and in excellent condition. Albert went to school, studied every night, and worked

Albert's Journey

as hard as he could to support himself. During the school year Albert continued to excel in his athletic ability along with the other members of the team. He knew that this year might be his last for varsity football because when a student reached 21 he could no longer play high school level sports. During one game of the Coast League Conference the Poly Tech varsity team faced off against San Diego.

The Poly varsity team met the San Diego players in the deciding game of the Coast League Conference in 1935. The Jackrabbits, as they were called, desired to bring the championship home to Poly Tech in a game that showed the strength and courage often celebrated in stories and movies about famous sports contests. However, the Jackrabbits were seven points ahead when San Diego made an early touchdown. Poly responded with another six points to even the score at halftime. It was then that one of Albert's team players, Walter McCowen, made a

San Diego – Pasadena Game 1935

Dolores A. Kelly

stunning dash of 80 yards, from his own 20-yard line until he crossed the San Diego goal line to make the winning touchdown.

The next game was against the Pasadena ball club. In the past, Albert and his Jackrabbit teammates always prepared for the Bulldog team defensively and offensively. However, preparation for this game was not necessary. The Jackrabbits considered the Pasadena team weak compared to their first-class squads of former years. Nevertheless, Albert's teammate Walter McCowen showed his abilities with runs of 83 yards and 21 yards for two touchdowns. Albert was so proud of this team and his teammates.

Albert's last game of the season was with Santa Ana – Glendale on November 17, 1935. The Poly Tech team traveled to Santa Ana and, as chronicled in the "Caerulea" 1935 yearbook, the team "set up a grid machine that turned out the most decisive score of the season." The Jackrabbits moved with force against the Saints, shutting them out 20 – 0. This was the last game of the Coast League and played on Thanksgiving Day, it showed the mighty Jackrabbits' power. The stadium crowd was about 7,500. This was truly a letdown for Glendale, but gave the mighty Jackrabbits the touchdowns they needed to run away with a victory. This was a great way for Albert to end his high school football career. He was ecstatic and felt he couldn't be more pleased than to have shared his Thanksgiving Day with teammates and a victory to boot.

Albert's graduation picture 1936

Chapter Six

After Graduation

Several of Albert's buddies had cars in high school, and they formed a car club. Of course, Albert did not have a car but the members wanted him to be a member of the club. So he joined the Totman's Car Club at Poly High School. All of the guys shared a wonderful friendship throughout their lives. After graduation, each one went into the business of repairing cars. There was Jack Parsons, who, a couple of years after he graduated owned a Shell Service Station and had a garage. George Marshall bought a Mobil Station with a garage. George Barlot became a mechanic for the city; he repaired police cars and fire trucks. Johnny Cassalino became a mechanic for Ford Motor Company, and eventually, Albert worked for General Motors Corporation on the assembly line building cars. These fellows remained the best of friends and stayed together throughout their adult lives.

In 1936, Albert graduated from high school and was desperately looking for a full-time position. He delivered papers, and continued to work at Hopi's Restaurant, washing dishes, cleaning floors – just anything to earn his meals and he did eat very well. The Hopi's made certain Albert always was well fed. He continued working at night in the bowling alleys setting up bowling pins. He would take any odd job he could find on the Long Beach Pike. He continued to collect milk glass bottles and turned them in for a penny apiece.

He wanted to live in an apartment or his own home. He had slept at the beach for a long time on a cot in a boat float, spent time on Mrs. Hunter's front porch and, now, because he was out of school, he wanted to devote his time to earning a living and providing for himself and a future. He loved this country because it offered so much, and because he was an immigrant it was important that Albert really belong in his community. He took the important step in May 1939, becoming a citizen of the United States of America. He was so proud to become an American citizen and was eager to learn as much about his country as he could. His curiosity was unstoppable. He promised to himself that he would travel to every corner and nook of the country to see its unparalleled beauty.

Albert worked as a lifeguard during the

Albert's Journey

summer months, but as the season ended he found a full-time job on the assembly line at General Motors Corporation. However, each summer, General Motors would shut down to retool its plants for the upcoming new model lines of cars. Albert didn't want to be left out in the cold without a job so he continued to be a lifeguard during the summer months.

The picture below represents the Long Beach lifeguards on August 12, 1939. Among these young men, six became firefighters. They were Harold King, Albert DeFrank, Henry Graef, Vernon Bond, John Olson, and Lorin Peck. Albert's picture is first row, second from left.

Long Beach Life Guards, August 12, 1939

Albert was very athletic. He constantly did tricks and athletic moves on the paddleboard in the Colorado Lagoon. He was acutely self-conscious of his size. He wanted to make certain he was always physically fit and ready for anything that would come along, whether it be saving a life at the beach or working hard providing for himself to survive any type of situation.

Albert on a paddleboard in the Colorado Lagoon

On July 4, 1940, Albert met the love of his life. Her name was Dorothy. She had taken a ride with her mother and some friends and it was a typical hot summer holiday. All Dorothy wanted to do was go down to the beach to take a swim. At that time she lived one block away from the Colorado Lagoon. She went down and stood under the palm tree on the beach and was speaking with friends. Albert was out on the lifeguard float in the middle of the lagoon talking with Carl Mills, a friend from high school. Albert saw Dorothy on the beach and said to Carl, "Do you see that girl?" Carl said, "Yes." Albert said, "She's going to be the mother to my children."

Albert's Journey

Carl told him he was full of gibberish. Carl said, "Al, you don't even know her!"

Carl, was the all-around teaser, said, "You can't even get a date with her," adding, "I bet you a dollar you can't get a date with her." Al agreed to the bet and said, "OK, I'll bet you a buck."

Albert and Carl returned to the beach and, without warning, Albert claimed that someone out in the water needed assistance. He went running by Dorothy and took his sunglasses off and said to her, "Will you hold these?" He continued to run down the beach and dove into the water and went out and made the rescue. Even now, Dorothy still doesn't know whether this was a set up or if it was an actual rescue. Yet, Dorothy continued to hold Albert's glasses for him until he came back. When he returned to the beach, he was very sweet and spoke with Dorothy and wanted to know if he could take her to a show the following night. She accepted happily.

He also wanted to know where she lived and she told him a block away from the lagoon. No doubt, Albert won the bet with Carl. Albert would do anything to make a nickel, and a buck certainly was nothing to turn down.

That was the beginning of Albert and Dorothy on the 4th of July 1940. Albert was 24 and Dorothy was 16.

Albert getting ready for his big day with friends

They only knew each other for 52 days before they were on their way to spending a lifetime of happiness together. They wanted to get married immediately. Just before Albert met Dorothy he had moved into an apartment with a close friend who shared the household expenses.

Neither Albert nor Dorothy had any idea how they could be married. Neither one had anything. Dorothy's mother didn't have anything to give to the couple. They talked it over and Albert said he had good friends from high school. One was Jack Parsons who owned a service station, so they stopped and talked with him. Albert told Jack that he and Dorothy were going to get married, but neither knew quite how they would pull this off. They thought about going to Las Vegas, Nevada. Jack had a beautiful car and he said, "If you want to go to Las Vegas I'll drive you because I want to see you get married, and you're going to go in style!" He had a new Packard convertible and insisted on driving Albert and Dorothy. He couldn't believe Albert was getting married. So, Jack and his girlfriend picked up Albert and Dorothy, and Dorothy's mother because the soon-to-be bride was underage and needed her mother's consent. Dorothy and Albert rode in the back seat traveling in the best possible style of the early 1940s. No question they were destined to be great friends forever.

Although Dorothy's mother was concerned about her marrying so young, she thought the world of Albert from the moment she met him. Jack Parsons passed the word around to all of

Albert feeling exhilarated before taking his vows

their friends. He said, "Hey, Al DeFrank is going to get married." Other friends of Albert's did not believe that he was going to get married, so they decided to go along with Jack to Las Vegas to see the proof directly.

Two carloads went to Las Vegas. Albert wanted to be married by a priest in the Catholic Church, but they would not marry them because Dorothy was not a Catholic. It seemed for every turn there was a problem. They talked it out and decided to go to the Justice of the Peace and were married down in the cellar of a courthouse in Las Vegas.

August 25, 1940

Albert's Journey

Walking out from the ceremony, Dorothy remembers her friends scraping the dirty rice off the steps and throwing it at them. Dorothy laughs about it and says, "This was first class!" Albert and Dorothy were married on August 25, 1940. Dorothy turned 17 the very next day.

Their friends took pictures of the great event and, as Dorothy tells the story today she smiles broadly, remembering the beginnings of a long, happy life with Albert. She still recalls clearly how they then went home to Dorothy's mother to live for the first month of their marriage. They had scraped enough money together to rent an apartment out in North Long Beach for a couple of months. Dorothy says the apartment's rent was $27 a month – not a small sum even in 1940. Their first home was a comfortable duplex apartment but it was very far from friends and the newlyweds often were very lonely in North Long Beach. Dorothy didn't know anyone so they decided to move closer to friends. They managed to find another apartment closer to their friends and family, which made both of them very happy.

Albert continued working as a summer lifeguard, making $28 a week. Also he remained at General Motors on the assembly line, making $35 a week. Albert and Dorothy thought their new life together was good and always getting better.

CHAPTER SEVEN

Grown Up and Starting A Family

Soon afterward, Dorothy suggested they find another duplex, a one-bedroom apartment at 1202 Dawson Street, Long Beach, and she remembered that they lived there for seven years. During that period Albert and Dorothy had two children. The first was a girl, Dolores, but they mostly called her Dee Dee. As if to celebrate that fateful meeting exactly one year earlier, Dee Dee was born on July 4, 1941. The second was named Dan who was born July 30, 1944. Even in 2005, Dorothy was ecstatic in recalling the days when they started their family: "I had Dee Dee nine months and one weekend after our marriage." There was no doubt about the evidence that Albert and Dorothy were so much in love. More than sixty years later, Dorothy talks with a loving smile about the early days she and Albert enjoyed in starting their family.

Dorothy explains, "It was unbelievable, when

Albert went to the hospital when Dee Dee was born. The nurse said to Albert, 'you have the prettiest baby in the nursery.' And, Albert said, 'I know.' He then went out and bought a pound box of See's Candy and took it to the nurse." Dorothy remembered a pound of candy at See's was 98 cents at that time and it was a lot of money then, but Albert thought it was well worth it.

Returning home with the baby, Dorothy washed all her diapers. They did not have disposables then as they do now. With washtubs and a scrub board, she washed diapers and Albert would hang them out on the clothesline and the fellows next door would razz and taunt Albert, calling him funny names. He didn't care. He was so proud when Dee Dee was born. He was so proud of their baby girl that he would do anything regardless of how others saw him.

Dorothy with Dee Dee and Dan

Albert's Journey

Dorothy declared that both she and Albert were so skinny and in love. It had been the storybook version of love at first sight, and they happily scrimped and saved pennies to place in their money jar. One day Albert lost his wallet with all the money they owned. However, they thanked the good Lord they had the penny jar. Dorothy had to roll pennies to take to the grocery store to purchase their weekly needs until another paycheck came. She remembered that toward the end of the week she bought three heads of cabbage for seven cents. They had cabbage and more cabbage – boiled, fried, in bacon fat, and coleslaw. They both continued to love cabbage even many years later. She says, "I look back and those first years were so very hard. I think we didn't have much of anything materialistic, but they were our happiest years. Our home was always full of laughter because there was always something to laugh about."

Albert had two ex-school friends who lived next door: brothers George and Carl Barlow. Carl went on to be a policeman, and George was a mechanic for the city of Long Beach. Dorothy recalled, "We had a wonderful friend and former classmate, Johnny Cassalino. Those three fellows would come over and play cards at our house. A lot of times I would try to make something for them, a hamburger or something. There was always something going on and there was never a dull moment. It was a happy, happy, happy time."

Albert continued to work as a lifeguard during the summer months, while also working a full-time job for General Motors on the assembly line in South Gate. General Motors would always shut down every summer to retool for the upcoming new model lines of cars. Albert didn't want to be idle and not have a job so lifeguarding continued to be his income during the long summer months.

Lifeguarding was a fun job for Albert because he loved the ocean and warm weather. He was always there if someone needed him.

However, Albert returned to work at the General Motors Plant when the assembly line

Albert carrying his buoy

Albert's Journey

was ready to roll out the new cars each fall. This was a very good job and allowed Albert to make enough money for their needs, but the war was approaching fast and he decided to leave the plant. After the Pearl Harbor attack in 1941, General Motors decided to shut its operations to retool for the war. Albert decided to attend vocational school to train as a welder and was hired at the Long Beach Naval Shipyard as soon as he finished his training. He thought this would allow him to have a job and make more money, especially with his growing family.

After working in the shipyard Albert discussed with Dorothy the possibility of joining the fire department with his friend. He hated the thought of taking a cut in pay, yet felt the career and job security would pay off over the long term. Albert really wanted to make certain he could provide for himself and his family for their future. He considered purchasing a house, but the war was on and there wasn't anything suitable so they continued to save their money and hoped that the war would be over soon.

Even before he thought about joining the fire department, Albert decided to be a motorcycle patrolman. When he worked at General Motors he bought a motorcycle to go back and forth to work, and he kept thinking about being on the motorcycle patrol team. This way he would be out in the fresh air and it would be fun. However, he was not tall enough to qualify for the squad. So, when his best friend Harold went to work with the fire department, Albert thought it would be a good idea to do the same. For two years Albert did nothing but study and work out to prepare himself for the fire department's rigorous battery of tests and physicals.

Albert easily passed his written test and his oral exams but when he went in for his physical the doctor told him he was a quarter of an inch too short so therefore he could not be hired. This broke Albert's heart. Harold, his best friend, was already on the fire department.

Nevertheless, he decided that he was going to make the fire department staff. Albert found a doctor who had a stretching table. He would go two to three times per week and lay on the stretching table. There were belts that went around his chest, chin, and ankles. He would stretch and relax, and stretch and relax some more. This was very expensive at the time. Each doctor visit was two dollars and, where every penny counted, this was an extra burden on the family. When he finished working for the day, Albert would run for miles every night. He worked out regularly with all types of exercises and weights to build his body up until he was in perfect physical condition. He never gave up and continued with his workouts every day. He would jog for miles as well as work with weights, parallel bars, and anything he could use to build up his body and his stamina.

The doctor told Albert a person is taller in the morning than at night. Albert had a police friend and neighbor who said that when Albert took the written examination for the fire department he had a high score and the agility scores were just as high and he passed everything. His only worry and concern was his height. He needed to gain that ever-elusive quarter of an inch in order to be accepted into the department.

The time came once again when Albert made an appointment for his physical for the fire department. Don Wein, his neighbor, told Albert, "I will take you, and when you get out of bed just get dressed, and when you come out to the car, lay on the back seat." When he arrived to take the physical Albert had some concern, but he passed. The doctor put him on the scale and measured Albert's height and the doctor said, "you're right on the line for acceptance." Finally, Albert was hired and inducted into the fire department in 1942.

Albert and Dorothy had a circle of friends they kept all through the years: Harold and Bernice King, Carl and Gladys Mills, Jack and Beth Hunt, and Johnny and Georgia Olsen. Dorothy commented fondly how "there were five women palling around with these firemen and we were all pregnant at the same time.

The fellows played basketball, they were on the softball team, and all of us would show up at the same time and watch the games." Dorothy was sure they received a lot of attention, and they did have a great time together. Once Dan was born in 1944, Albert and Dorothy knew their family was complete.

Yet, Dorothy started to show signs of being worried. She had read and was concerned about the fact that a child who has been abused will abuse their children, but that was not always true. Albert would never abuse his children or think of doing it. He would call Dorothy in when one of the kids would do something wrong. He would say, "Dot, I think you'd better give him a swat on the butt." Dorothy would say, "No, Al, that's not the way." Albert would then say, "Well I feel like giving him a swat on the butt, but I'm afraid it may be too hard." Instead, he would say things to Dee Dee and Dan that would hurt their feelings, so he would get his message across. In retrospect, Dorothy thought that maybe a swat on the butt would have been easier than hurting their feelings. However, throughout both Dee Dee and Dan's life, Albert kept his promise without fail. He NEVER struck his children or raised his hand. He talked with them and they knew when he was angry and when not to do certain things.

Dee Dee explained that she always tried to be good because she never wanted her dad to be upset with her. She says, "I hated to get in trouble, I knew if I did something wrong I would be punished. That fear kept me out of trouble (most of the time) and I followed the rules. When Dad spoke, I listened. I listened real good when the vein on his forehead stuck out. I knew exactly what to do: keep my mouth shut."

Dee Dee called to mind how she learned to understand how her Dad tried to be a good teacher and parent. "He wanted us to be perfect, which we weren't. When we did something wrong he would lecture us. This usually happened at the dinner table. To make a point he would pound the table and the silverware would rattle and he had our attention."

On a lighter side Dee Dee realized that her dad wasn't perfect. Dorothy made a salad one evening for dinner and it was in a Tupperware container with a lid; he picked it up to mix the salad and thought he would entertain the family by lifting it over his head to shake. To everyone's surprise including Albert's the lid was not on tight and he sat there dripping in salad. They all had a good laugh.

Dee Dee reminisces about her father wanting to give both she and her brother Dan everything he didn't have when he was young, which was a close loving family, and he did with great success. He worked hard for the family and let everyone know that his family came first. She says, "Dad was honest, hard working and very competitive. He always said exactly what he was thinking. His words were never sugar coated." Even after many years Dee Dee remembers one of his most frequent sayings:" You show me a good loser and I'll show you an idiot."

Albert's Journey

Dee Dee reflects that when she and Dan were young their dad wasn't home much. He was working two and three jobs to make extra money because their mom was sick and needed expensive medicine. When he was home he had to be "mom." Dee Dee remembers when he tried to brush her hair, cook, and shop for the family needs. He wasn't too good at any of those tasks, but he always tried to do his best. He took Dee Dee shopping for new shoes and made her buy Buster Brown boys shoes because he thought they would not wear out as quickly as girls shoes on the asphalt playground. Dee Dee reminisced, "I tried really hard to wear out those shoes fast."

Albert also fixed dinner and he loved to use only one pan. He put all the leftovers together to heat. Dan and Dee Dee were relieved when their mom was better and took over the cooking duties. They all remembered those leftover meals and they couldn't wait for their mom to be well again, especially for a new menu at the dinner table. However, they always did laugh quite a bit at Dad's creative cooking techniques and with that it always was something good to remember, no matter how the food tasted.

Chapter Eight

Friends, Family, and Camping Trips

Albert had no trouble making friends. He could walk into a room and meet everyone and feel as though he knew them. Dorothy said, "He never met a stranger." Dorothy could sit and tell countless stories about Albert helping every person that he ever met. Even after many years, Albert's closest friends remained Harold King and Carl Mills. Harold and Albert's friendship had started on the beach. Yes, they had begun their friendship with a challenge to fight, and they wrestled, horse played, and carried on all their lives. Harold was taller by one inch, but he easily outweighed Albert. Meanwhile, Albert stayed slim all his life. Harold plumped up and always had to go on diets.

In 1945, Albert became the engineer on the fireboat in the Long Beach Harbor. His captain was Kenny Miller. Kenny loved to fish and they would take the fireboat out in the ocean while they were on duty.

Officially, they said that they were out on inspection but they, unofficially, were out cruising and fishing at the same time. Kenny Miller and his wife Pat would occasionally take their fishing boat up to the High Sierras and stay at June Lake. Kenny thought Albert was outstanding and took him under his wing. He knew Albert's background and gave him a lot of credit for getting where he was.

One day Albert came home from work and said, "Dot, we have been invited to go with Pat and Kenny. I think I can get three days off work. Can you get your mother to come over to stay with the kids?" Dan was a year old and Dee Dee was four. Dorothy said, "I hate to leave the kids." Albert agreed and stated, "I do, too, but we can't take them up there. We'll have to go and we will follow Pat and Kenny up in the mountains because he wants us to fish with him."

Albert's Journey

Albert really wanted to go, but Dorothy didn't. However, she said, "I'll see if mom can get off work to stay with the kids for three days." Dorothy didn't have the right type of clothes to go up into the Sierras in October, but she was able to get a few things together. Dorothy's mom had said, "Yes, she would come and stay with the kids."

Albert was very happy about going up to the

Albert and Kenny at June Lake

Sierras with Kenny and Pat. Kenny had extra fishing poles because Albert and Dorothy did not have any fishing equipment, and Dorothy told Albert, "I feel so funny, I don't even know that lady." Pat was several years older than Dorothy. Kenny had met Dorothy a couple of times, yet Dorothy still felt out of place. She found it hard to get rid of the doubts about going on the trip. The big day finally came and Albert and Dorothy followed Kenny and Pat up to June Lake on the June Lake Loop in the High Sierras. They were in snowstorms, it rained, and Dorothy was cold. She didn't have the proper clothes for the trip but Kenny's wife Pat came to her rescue. She gave Dorothy long johns to put on as well as an extra blanket. They took care of them as though they were their father and mother because they dearly loved Albert.

Kenny and Pat took Dorothy out in their boat to fish one morning and were caught in a terrible storm with plenty of thunder and lightning. Dorothy was scared to death. However, Dorothy caught fish and thought this was great and from then on, Albert and Dorothy were hooked on traveling up to the High Sierras. During the first trip with Kenny and Pat, they stayed in a cabin three days: a very small place with many cracks, allowing the wind to flurry throughout the log cabin. It was difficult for Albert and Dorothy because their clothes were barely enough to

Albert's Journey

withstand the windy wintry-like conditions.
 On the morning they were to leave for home a flash flood in the town of Mohave washed out

the highway. Albert called to find out about the conditions of the Tioga Pass through Yosemite but it apparently was closed because of heavy snow. They were stuck and could not get home. Albert contacted the forest department and found they couldn't go home even through Reno, Nevada because of the snow. They were resigned to the fact that they couldn't leave the Sierras. They were stuck. Dorothy was just sick, because she knew her mother was supposed to go to work the next day. Dorothy called her mom and said, "Mom, I know you won't believe me, but I can't get home. We're flooded out one way and snowed in the other." Dorothy's mother said, "We'll work it out somehow."

Finally, the next day they had a detour on a road that leveled off through the Mohave and they went back over Route 395, taking a cutoff instead of going through the town of Mohave. They headed toward San Bernardino and saw a Greyhound bus that had overturned off the highway and was buried in mud halfway up the windows. The flood in the desert was unbelievable. It was a flash mud flood that seemed unreal, almost mythical. That was Albert and Dorothy's first time in the High Sierras, a clearly unforgettable event.

Through the following year, Albert and Dorothy managed to buy poles and equipment to go fishing. Albert said, "Dot, we will never

Albert's Journey

leave the kids again," and they never did. They managed to borrow a tent and they had their fishing gear, taking Dee Dee and Dan even when the boy was just two years old. At age 60 Dan was still enjoying many memories of the time with the family in the High Sierras.

Dan narrates the story of when he was ten or 11 years of age, sometime in the 1950s and the family was camping on Grant Lake, California, about 100 miles from Carson City. The wind was coming up and it was getting stormy, and while out in the boat Albert and Dan either ran out of gas or had motor trouble. Dan couldn't remember specifically what happened but either way the motor on the fishing boat had stopped. Albert told Dan everything was going to be all right, but the lake was getting very rough, so Albert started rowing against the wind as darkness began to fall. Dan said that they usually stopped fishing before it became dark. However, instead of motoring back to the other side of the lake where the car was parked, Albert had to row across the lake against the wind. As the lake got rougher Albert said in a calming voice, "Dan, everything is going to be alright." Dan felt safe even in the midst of what was happening. They did make it back to shore, and Albert had rowed the boat against the wind the entire length of the lake because they were at the far end when the motor stopped. Dorothy and Albert's friend

Kenny Miller were there because they became worried when they did not get back to camp in time. Reflecting on this incident Dan treasured how his father took charge and rowed against the windstorm.

Dan showed us that he was the best fisherman that day

Albert always made sure that everybody in the family would have a good time at camp. Dan explained, "When dad, Dee Dee, and I were hiking, Dee Dee was three years older, and sometimes I couldn't keep up." Dan remembered that his dad would place him on his shoulders because he was still quite young. They use

Albert's Journey

to camp for a month at a time at Lake Tenaya inside Yosemite National Park. Today, it still is a pristine lake – great for fishing, with beach access and a perfect area for picnics, day hikes and stargazing. Lake Tenaya is in North Central Sierra California, in Mariposa County along Highway 120 inside Yosemite. Those were some of the fondest memories Dan had, especially when they were out fishing.

When Dan was about eight years old, the family had a rubber raft and used the raft at Lake Tenaya. Dad would row because they didn't have a motor, and they would let the fishing lines out

Dan, Dee Dee, and Smoky at Lake Tenaya

and troll for trout. Dan remembers one night in particular. He caught two fish and thought he was the best fisherman on the lake. He was so proud. Albert rowed all over the lake and, the next day, Dorothy took a photograph of Dan with his fishing pole, showing two fingers in the air to signify that he had caught two fish. With this attitude and smirk on his face he thought he was some fisherman.

Lake Tenaya was a very remote spot. It was high up in the High Sierras, at about 9,000 feet. Albert, Dorothy, Dee Dee, and Dan had the rubber raft with them when they camped. The water in this area was shallow for quite some distance out from the banks before there was a drop-off. Albert would tie a rope to the rubber raft and secure it to shore and Dan would be attached as though he was on a leash. He had enough rope to row around, but would come to the end of the rope before he could reach the deep water. Once again, Dan felt proud that he was doing something out in this rubber raft all by himself.

Dee Dee recollects that growing up with dad was never dull. There was something going on all the time. Her parents were very fortunate to have good close friends who were more like family. They had children the same ages as Dan and Dee Dee and they all did things together. They had picnics at Irvine Park where they rented boats and paddled around the lake. Mom made giant lunches and they would eat all day. The kids climbed trees and caught pollywogs in the creek. Once a year they all went to the Firemen's Picnic where the DeFranks regularly won their share of the prizes.

Albert did everything to make the kids feel right at home in the mountains. Dee Dee says, "Dad always made me feel safe, secure, and loved." She knew he could take care of anything that could happen and he wasn't afraid of anything or anybody. For example, one night they were camping at Lake Tenaya and in their tent asleep when something hit the side of the tent hard. Albert jumped up, and after saying a few choice words, looked outside and saw a big bear. He picked up a board and chased him down to the beach. Dee Dee says, "I guess he thought he was Davy Crockett."

Whether the family camped in the Sierras or at Lake Tahoe, there were no dull moments, with Albert feeling as much like a kid as Dee Dee and Dan. Dee Dee remembered how "Dad always had as much fun playing as Dan and me. He loved water skiing, fishing, hiking, and playing any kind of game. I was happiest with my dad when we were on vacation. That was a time of family togetherness and one hundred percent fun."

The kids always looked to being as far away

as possible from civilization in the Sierras. Referring to the rubber boat much like the one shown in the picture above, Dee Dee said, "Dad would put his fishing pole between his feet. He would keep rowing and saying, 'Here fish, fish, fish, here fish, fish, fish.'"

Dee Dee also expressed that when he would take her hiking to places he probably shouldn't have, but they always endured. He would show her where to step and how to climb over and under the rocks. Like anything else, it was fun. As Dee Dee affirmed, "When Dan and I were teens we had family friends who had vacationed at Lake Tahoe and talked dad into going there instead of the back woods. After that first vacation to Lake Tahoe, Mom and Dad never wanted to go anywhere else."

Everyone played on the beach and water-skied all day. They sat around the campfire with friends or went to teen dances at night. It was a great life, Dee Dee declared, "I was always thankful that my parents enjoyed their vacations as much as Dan and me because I knew they scrimped and saved so they could afford to go and do all that they did."

Like his sister, Dan says that growing up and being the son of a firefighter was quite an experience. Most of their parents' friends were either firefighters or policemen. The firemen, especially, were a tight knit group; among them

Albert's Journey

were Carl and Gladys Mills, Harold and Bernice King, and Albert and Dorothy. Carl, Harold, and Albert were Long Beach lifeguards together and high school chums. From the time they were lifeguards they all went into the Long Beach Fire Department. Carl and Gladys had two daughters: one was Dee Dee's age, and the other was Dan's age. Harold and Bernice had three children. Diane was Dee Dee's age and Carlin's age while Don was about nine months older than Dan and then along came Bob.

For everybody, all of these people were like an extended family. Being the son of a firefighter was special because of the camaraderie among all the families. Any one of them could have called on the other for help and it would have been done without hesitation or another word spoken. As Dee Dee and Dan acknowledged, that was a wonderful atmosphere to grow up in with a lot of loving people.

The stories never seemed to stop. Dan recalls when the family went camping on Silver Lake, on the June Lake Loop about 120 miles from Carson City, Nevada. One day, Dan said, the trash men were coming through the campground and dad started a conversation with them. He found out that they were hungry. Mom was in the trailer cooking breakfast. He invited the strangers to get off their truck and come join them for a good camp breakfast, which included fried potatoes, eggs, and trout.

Even if one were a stranger with dad he would always be invited to sit down at the table with him and break bread.

In 1957 Albert had a 12-foot fishing boat and a 16-foot house vacation trailer and the family went on a fishing trip in the High Sierras and were camped on Silver Lake. One morning Harold and Bernice King and their children came by on their way to Lake Tahoe to go camping at Meeks Bay, which is on the west side of Lake Tahoe on the California side. Albert and Dorothy packed everything up and followed them up to the lake and went into Meeks Bay. They found many friends camping there, and that was Albert and Dorothy's beginning of camping at Meeks Bay. Al and the kids were introduced to water skiing and they loved it, and from then on they went every year. They were there every summer from 1957 to 1976.

Albert's Journey

Dan celebrated his birthday there on the 30th of July every year.

Dan turned 21 when they were camped there and the only thing he wanted to do was to go to the North Shore and play the slot machines. Albert and Dorothy agreed and they proceeded to the North Shore. They all had a great lunch and knew Dan was very careful about spending money. He bought a two-dollar roll of dimes and, on the fourth or fifth time, he pulled the machine and won $500. That was the beginning and the end of his playing the slots. He cashed in his winnings, converted them into a bank check and mailed it to the Long Beach Fire Department Credit Union to have the winnings deposited into his savings account. Albert and Dorothy thought — uh oh, this was bad — the first time he played the slot machines and won that he might be a gambler. Happily, he never was because he never cared for it. He worked at Harvey's and Harrah's Casino in security but never played the slot machines or gambled. Even today, he doesn't gamble or drink. Like Albert, he's just one really great guy.

The Meeks Bay adventures always brought out plenty of stories. In 1961 Dick and Dot Molden had been on a trailer trip and were gone for a couple of weeks. They heard about Meeks Bay and wanted to check it out, so they pulled into a trailer park and it was crowded. They did find a place to park and two fellows came over. One was Albert DeFrank and the other was Harold King. They noticed Dick's fireman sticker on his car, and said, "We clean windows for firemen."

Well, that was the first meeting. Harold and Albert took their Windex and washed all Dick's windows and introduced themselves. They then introduced their wives Bernice and Dorothy, and invited Dick and Dot to their campfire that night, resulting in a good time together. Every year the couples went back at the same time and soon formed a circle of friends at Meeks Bay. The group included Bob Taylor, Hubie Kenda (another Long Beach firefighter) and his wife Lolly, Harold and Bernice King, and Carl and Gladys Mills. It seemed that the circle of friends widened continuously.

Good vacation habits were certainly hard to break. The next year Dick and Dot Molden went up to Meeks Bay again and ran into the same group of people. They became yet closer and Albert had a ski boat and taught Dick and his daughter how to ski. He would offer to teach anyone who wanted to learn. They would all go into town once in a while and gamble together and, at least once a week, they all went into the Cal-Neva Club in Nevada for a luncheon and a bingo game, which everyone enjoyed very much.

Later, usually in September, Hubie Kendal and his wife, Lolly, would have a backyard barbeque

Albert's Journey

and they invited all the Tahoe gang. With time passing they all had a much closer relationship. Then Dick and Dot purchased a lot in San Clemente and in 1974 they built a house. The day they moved in Albert and Dorothy came by with a surprise and told them they purchased a house up the street just about a half block away. From then on, Albert and Dorothy spent a great deal of time with Dick and Dot Molden. They all went to the beach almost every day for the longest time together and went to Loft Land several times.

Dee Dee remembered that Dick and Dot lived near mom and dad for 13 years. They always felt as though they were on vacation that entire time. Dorothy confirmed the many stories of the wonderful times she and Albert had with Dick and Dot. They went on trips every winter up to Lake Tahoe and spent a few days in the snow because they all just loved the area.

While in San Clemente at the beach the couples discovered rocks offshore almost one half mile off the beach and Albert would like to swim out there every day. Dick Molden recalled one incident, much to the chagrin of the lifeguards who didn't want Al out there because they thought he was too old, and that there were a lot of seals out there and seals were the favorite food for sharks. Apparently, one day Al swam out about a half a mile and he lost his dentures, but he dove and dove until he found them and brought them back to tell his story for all to hear. Everyone – even the lifeguards – had the biggest laugh with that story.

Albert's character never wavered on land or on water. Once, in San Clemente, Al had some work done on his Ford truck and when he looked at the bill he saw a charge for miscellaneous expenses that came to five or ten percent of the bill. It covered shop towels, car keys, grease and so forth.

Al didn't like the idea of being charged for these items on his bill. According to Dick Molden who tells the story, "Albert told the dealer 'I didn't just get off the boat; you can't charge me for things like this!' The serviceman and the manager in charge said, Well, it's that or nothing.' Well, Al said, 'Then it's nothing'. He stomped out of the dealership and didn't pay and never returned."

With Albert and Dorothy, friendships were meant for a lifetime. While living in San Clemente, Dick and Dot continued to go on many day trips and vacations with the happy couple. They would go in the wintertime and travel up to Lake Tahoe, California, and gamble on the Nevada side and play bingo as well. Later, they moved on to Lake Powell, and then on to Grant Lake several times. While living in San Clemente, not far from the San Diego area, and after they first moved into

Albert's Journey

the area the whole group of them were constant traveling companions. Bob and Marylou Flood lived across the street. Dick and Dot Molden – along with Albert and Dorothy – did many things together as a trio of couples along with Bob Taylor who then was the South Gate police chief.

As the years passed, Meeks Bay had changed and so did the experience of camping there. The owner sold out and it was under different management. The camping spaces were cut down and Dorothy and Albert and the rest of the gang stopped going to Meeks Bay. Albert and Dorothy then started to go up to Grant Lake twice a year where they enjoyed trout fishing. While Dorothy and Albert were at Grant Lake, Dick and Dot Molden took their trailer up and spent a lot of time fishing and exploring the territory around that area. Dorothy was a fantastic cook, especially with fresh trout. It didn't take much for Dick and Dot to go over to their trailer and have a big beautiful trout dinner.

And, water-skiing became a favorite pastime. Dorothy passed on it but Albert and the kids always joined in the fun. In the first year, Carl Mills had a ski boat at the time and pulled them along, but the following year when they went back they had a beautiful brand new custom-built ski boat with a mercury motor. Everybody in the family seemed to be hooked on Lake Tahoe and water skiing. It turned out that the family would rather water ski than eat and Dorothy had quite a job at getting them to stop at the end of the day to come in for dinner. At Meeks Bay at Tahoe, there was a campfire and at 11 p.m. there was a camp rule that the firemen had buckets of water to make sure that every spark was out. When they were sure everyone could go to bed.

The summers of camping and water-skiing were at the center of the best time for the "fire family" as everyone knew their firefighter friends. But, new people were always coming into the family, like Dick and Dot Molden who were living at the time in Downey, California. Others came from Santa Rosa, California and Al was eager to teach everyone to water ski, as he just thought it was the greatest thing. Up until this day, all of these people remained dear friends. Those who are still alive continue to visit. As Dorothy says, "I feel like we have always been so lucky and so rich with friends we have had the best."

CHAPTER NINE

A Chosen Career

Earlier Albert had considered training to become a motorcycle patrolman, and while working at General Motors he bought a motorcycle to go back and forth to work. As we learned earlier, Albert – after much work and exercise – finally became a member of the Long Beach Fire Department. From that happy day in 1942 when he officially became a firefighter, Albert took a strong interest in the history of the department. Below is a small portion of the history of the Long Beach Fire Department.

The Long Beach Fire Department

For Albert, learning as much as he could about the fire department was as important as discovering his family's history. It was among his many great passions. The Long Beach Fire Department was formally known as the

Albert's Journey

Willmore, and, on March 16, 1897, a group of citizens realized that in order to reduce the number of fires and loss of property, it was time to establish a Volunteer Fire Department. The Board of Trustees approved funds for a hand-drawn ladder truck that carried axes, buckets made of leather, and many other items used to douse fires. All of the equipment was housed in a building in the alley between Ocean Avenue and First Street, Pine and Pacific Avenues in Long Beach. Many fundraisers were held over the years to raise money for the purchase of helmets, shirts, belts, and other necessary items for the members. It's hard for us now to think that such an essential city service such as firefighting was made possible by volunteers and by fundraisers.

Hand drawn ladder truck
1890 Rumsey Hand Drawn Ladder Truck

Dolores A. Kelly

December 2, 1901: Two small hose carts were purchased by the trustees of the city. The picture is below.

Carts were equipped with 500 feet of hose

Albert's Journey

1924 Ahrens-Fox Pumper

1924 Ahrens-Fox Front View

Dolores A. Kelly

Morgan Smoke Hood Circa 1900s

Amoskeg 1907 Dorse Drawn Steam Pumper

Albert's Journey

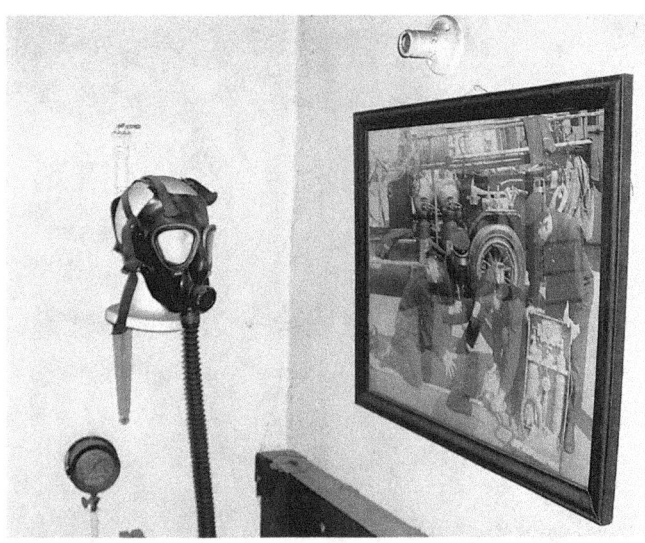

Mask attached to a rescue air pump circa 1950s

1935 GMC panel truck used as First Aid/Salvage

Dolores A. Kelly

Badge display Donated by Ray Chambers

Long Beach Fire Department Helmets Circa 1930s

Albert's Journey

Uniforms donated from Australia, England, Germany

Dolores A. Kelly

*Acceptance Test of a Fire Department Pumper
Circa 1920s*

Albert's Journey

Firefighting in Long Beach at the turn of the century was much different than it is today. Going back more than a hundred years, we learn that the city finally purchased a large bell along with 35 fire hydrants. This would become the nucleus of the fire department and it would grow along with the city, which was expanding rapidly with new residents and new buildings. Prior to 1902, all men and youth who were able bodied became firemen when needed. Merchants declared a half-day holiday and closed up shop whenever there was a major blaze in the city.

However, between 1900 and 1907, the Board of Trustees began to acknowledge the need for a permanent firefighting organization. On May 27, 1902, the Board gave the green light to organize the first fire department in Long Beach, especially since it had become a city. During that same year the department published a book and the individual pictures of all its members of the fire department were featured. The reason why there was no group picture was the chief, at that time, wanted all the members to be dressed alike so the members all used the same coat. This was the only uniform coat that was used in the department in 1902.

Albert's future employer – even long before he was born in faraway Italy – continued to grow in the first years of the new century. In 1908 the fire department was now managed just like the police department. In 1911 the first motor driven pumper called "A Robinson" was purchased. By 1912 the city had grown to a population of 30,000. It would even be much larger when Albert came to California.

Even years later when Albert finally made the department, he wanted to know as much as possible about the story of how the fire department grew to be what he would see when he finally was accepted in 1942. In 1917 there were 36 members who staffed the four fire stations and many were about to leave to enlist in the military because of World War I. However, the population had grown to 44,865 citizens and was still climbing rapidly. So, in 1920, 25 additional men were added bringing the total to 60 firemen and the construction of two more fire stations were underway. Over the years the budget kept increasing until 1929 when the stock market crash brought hard economic times. Like the rest of the United States, unemployment was a major problem in Long Beach.

The Long Beach Fire Department also fell on hard times. In 1929 the No. 12 Station was built, but it was unoccupied until 1936. Station No. 8 was ready to be occupied, but was not opened until later. Things started to improve in

Albert's Journey

1930 and the city had engineers to drive and pump the pumpers and auto firemen to drive the trucks, chemical trucks and tillers. When 1931 came around city officials took steps to improve the fire and police pension system, something that would benefit every employee – including Albert – in his later years.

Of course, Long Beach – like any other California community – had to deal with the prospect that at some point an earthquake would hit the area. In 1933 a major earthquake struck the area, the one described earlier in this book. It occurred on March 10, 1933 and it was recorded at 5:54 p. m. Pacific Standard Time. The initial shock was a magnitude of 6.3 and rumbled for 11 seconds. The epicenter was located just a few miles off shore from Newport Beach beneath the Pacific Ocean. There were numerous aftershocks, both mild and severe. Four fire stations were demolished and others badly shaken, but they were still occupied.

Although many of the fire stations were damaged, the firemen continued to pursue fires and rescue calls to dig people out. Two fires developed to serious proportions: one was in the oil fields and the other was in the chemistry building at Polytechnic High School, Albert's alma mater. Below are some photos taken after the quake.

*Lynwood Tank. Collapse in shock of March 10, 1933.
(J. B. Macelwane Archives, Saint Louis University)*

*"South Gate. 150,000 gallon tank collapsed
March 10, 1933 Shock Long Beach."
(J. B. Macelwane Archives, Saint Louis University)*

Albert's Journey

*Damage to the Long Beach Polytechnic High School.
Photo from H.M. Engle.*

*Looking at the damage to the Long Beach
Polytechnic High School Auditorium.
Photo from H.M. Engle.*

"Long Beach, California, Earthquake March 10, 1933, killed 120 people, with hundreds injured and about $40 million in damages.

The epicenter was located just offshore near Newport Beach, Magnitude 6.3 at 5:54 p.m." (Engle, 1933).

By the time Albert arrived in California, Long Beach had grown significantly from its much smaller days 30 years earlier. At this time, the city's population was about 150,000 and covered an area of some 29 square miles. The city was mainly residential but the petroleum industry was the greatest fire hazard. As the population increased so did the city services to the community. The fire department increased the number of men on the fire department. With another global war fast approaching, it was inevitable that the country would become entangled at any moment in the international conflict.

In 1942, the same year that Albert joined the department, the firefighters would receive special training and the city decided that new men and new equipment were needed. This included training on how to deal with chemical warfare, with training provided by the fire battalion chief and fire captain who had received their own training at Fort McArthur. Even Albert would see the chemical warfare instructional manual. Albert was proud that his department had been praised by high-ranking army officers who were confident that the fire department could handle any crisis or disaster. The memories of the attack on Pearl Harbor at Hawaii were fresh

Albert's Journey

*An interior court. Polytechnic High School, Long Beach. March 10, 1933
(J. B. Macelwane archives, Saint Louis University)*

Earthquake damage. Ground failures. Long Beach, Ca. Photo by Mr. Cortelyou, Engineer, California Division of Highways, L.A. District.

in everybody's minds, especially those who lived along the ocean coastline in California.

In 1942 the first fireboat, the "Charles S. Windham" was placed into service on May 8. Albert was not hired until August 1942. Yet he was fascinated by every detail of the department's new prized purchase. The boat, docked at El Embarcadero near Pier D, engaged on harbor patrol duty from dark until daylight depending upon the Coast Guard having adequate services for patrol activities. The span of the Windham was 35.1 feet. The model, a Chrysler Marine with 115 horsepower, with a centrifugal pump type, was assigned to Station No. 15.

The population in Long Beach was growing rapidly and in 1943 reached 236,336. Albert would work at various types of stations throughout the years. He was assigned to the ambulance and drove the city ambulance for a

couple of years, moved up to auto fireman, and chauffeured the fire chief for quite some time.

Albert was elated when he was stationed on the fireboat during World War II in Long Beach Harbor.

Albert is first from right

Albert experienced piloting the fireboat and enjoyed that immensely. When on duty in the fireboat he was the engineer, and his captain, Kenny Miller, was one of his closest friends. They cemented their friendship, and Kenny

Auto Fireman

brought along a couple of fishing poles aboard the fireboat. Together, he and Albert managed to get in a little fishing while they were in the

Albert, right, along with his other buddies on the fireboat

Albert's Journey

harbor. They would be on standby, and when they dropped that fishing line in the water Kenny said, "I used hot dogs, marshmallows, and bacon fat – anything that I could put on the hook that was bait, as any good fireman would use."

In 1943 Long Beach Fire Department's Drill Class honored 14 of its finest, including Albert. The picture below from left to right features names of those honored in the first row then the second row. Albert is first row third from left.

LBFD - Drill School - Class of 1943
1st row - L to R Jim Frame, Ken Elliott, Al DeFrank, Geo Magrudder, Everett Sanier,
Clyde Wilcott - Ernest Steiner, Drill Master
2nd Row LtoR - Fred Porter, Bill Moffitt, Carl Mills, Al Mole, Oscar Steffen, Dick Calmyer

Since Albert's induction into the fire department was in 1942 he was considered to have been covered under the old plan, which did not increase his pension. But, with his strong work ethic intact as ever, he worked for half the pay for ten years extra. He loved his job and didn't want to leave so he invested more time into the department. It didn't matter to Albert, he couldn't give up his job. He loved his work so much that it made him a happy person, and working for half pay didn't displease or disappoint him one bit. He went from fireman, to auto fireman, and then onto engineer.

August 7, 1946
Albert demonstrated the nozzle pressure

In 1948 he was coaxed to take the captain's exam, but he really didn't want the rank. He said, "I'd be a captain and I'd be between the men and the officers and I wouldn't be happy that way.

Albert's Journey

I would try to please the officers and the men under me." Albert loved what he was doing and where he was stationed. He was stationed at Fire Station No. 16. He just wanted to stay an engineer. He enjoyed his work as an engineer, and drove the crash truck at the airport. A crash truck is an emergency vehicle stationed at an airport and equipped and designed to save lives in the event of an airplane crash.

He enjoyed driving all the equipment and was so proud of all he had accomplished in the department. All the equipment was kept in showcase condition; everything had to be perfect. He was fastidious about everything he did. Dorothy says, "If you stood still you got dusted off, polished or waxed."

Long Beach Municipal Airport Fire Station No. 16

Dolores A. Kelly

Years after the war, the United States Air Force finally moved out of its installation at the Long Beach Airport, which meant the city would now have more responsibility for the fire facility. To meet the city's needs a Yankee Crash Truck from the Yankee Manufacturing Company was purchased and positioned at the Long Beach

June 16, 1961
Apparatus # 161 Location Long Beach Airport

Crash Truck 1961 Yankee Manufacturing Company

Albert's Journey

1961 Yankee Test to put out fire required by FAA

Airport, Station No. 16.

When Albert left the fireboat he was made engineer and briefly continued with the fire department at Station No.11. This was in North Long Beach and then he was transferred out to the Long Beach Airport Station No.16 and drove the crash truck. Oh, how Albert loved his job driving the crash truck. He kept saying, "I'm

the captain on the gravy train." The crash truck, one of the largest pieces of fire equipment in the state of California, was all Albert's responsibility. While in the department there were two crash trucks. The manufacturer came to the site and trained Albert on the vehicle.

Nevertheless, there was a caper in the firehouse about Al because he was so short that a fellow firefighter named William Tommy Jones who was over six feet routinely picked up Albert to put him on the truck. This was a routine that Tommy and the brother firefighters immensely enjoyed. All of his firefighter brothers got a laugh out of this practice.

Albert was a very positive person about everything. He loved to argue and would argue with anyone. However, Dorothy would not argue with him. She disagreed with him on some things, but he always thought he won every argument or problem because he could bellow the loudest. Dorothy felt assured and protected because he was an excellent provider who loved and revered his family, and took very good care of them. His honesty was always solid and he happened to be confident at all times because he consistently believed in himself.

Albert had a talent for tackling any problem, small or large. He was an avid reader and used every chance he had. It was a joke at the fire department that when Albert received his

Albert's Journey

Reader's Digest he would read it from cover to cover, and take the digest with him to the fire station every morning. One of the firefighters drew this caricature of Albert. No one really knows who drew it but whoever did created the picture as a good-natured razz for Al about his passion for Readers' Digest magazines and for being one of the shortest people to drive the

A fellow worker drew this caricature of Albert at the fire station

largest fire truck in all of California.

At every election, Albert voted like any responsible citizen. However, what bothered him was that the candidate he voted for in presidential races never won. Before every election, he gathered all the political information and every newspaper he could find with information regarding every candidate. He was registered as a Democrat and would collect all his "voter homework" and take it with him to the fire station. He and his buddies would read and scrutinize all the problems, discussing them at length and trying to decide whom to vote for in the upcoming election.

Meanwhile, Dorothy was registered as a Republican from the time she became old enough to vote, following her family members who were registered Republicans. She had traced her family tree as far back as George Washington and everyone had been a Republican. This didn't bother Albert. However, he once skipped both parties and registered as an Independent.

As clearly shown in the above caricature Albert had a "pop-off valve." Every time he would get riled up about a political issue a vein would pop out on his forehead and that would warn all those around him that he was ready to detonate on the issue. However, and happily so, this didn't occur too often. This became a popular joke around the firehouse. Here was the shortest guy

Albert's Journey

in the firehouse, driving the largest crash truck in the state and with a magnanimous personality – all of which made Albert a very popular man in and out of the fire department.

Albert was very proud of being an engineer for the department. One would never see him without a cloth in his hand. He constantly maintained everything, polishing and shining, barely if ever missing a step. When it was time to roll the equipment out of the fire station it definitely was ready to move.

He could have retired after 25 years of service, but he kept telling, his wife, Dorothy, "I love what I do."

*Albert DeFrank, Long Beach Fire Department
Hired 1942, Retired 1976*

However, it was difficult for him to slow down when he did retire. Dorothy stated, "It wasn't easy, since Al has only two speeds. Either he is flat on his back or full speed ahead. That was Al."

Albert remained with the fire department until August 1976. He didn't want to leave and wanted to work any position, but time made him retire. He kept telling Dorothy what a beautiful country the United States was, and that when he retired he wanted to travel all over America and see everything, which they did. They both managed to visit 49 states and had a great time. They were saving Hawaii for last but unfortunately, they never reached that destination.

Dorothy scanned through the many newspaper clippings Albert kept over the years. She pulled one that started, "City workers put dignity aside. Five thousand persons enjoyed a city employee picnic at Howelton Park"... and it goes on to report about all the wonderful food and down below it said Al DeFrank "is assured of a hot reception by the mates in the fire department when he reports for duty. He took first place in the men's leg contest."

Albert was always proud of winning the pretty leg contest, and took a generous amount of ribbing, but he felt it was more than worth it. Below is a picture of the Long Beach Fire Department family that was taken at the park after the fun and games.

Albert's Journey

Albert hardly ever sat in one spot for long. Dorothy recalls that during the war gasoline was rationed and Al signed up for a victory bicycle, but had to wait for quite some time. He received a letter that permitted him to purchase a bicycle. He rode his bike back and forth to work every chance he could. She remembered that they had been living near the Los Angeles Harbor and the Long Beach Harbor. There were several blackouts, the air raid sirens would blow, and he knew he had to get right to the fire station.

During the blackouts, Dorothy received her kiss goodbye, every time he left the house. He would get on the bike and pedal down to the harbor and onto the fireboat. She thought they lived at least ten to 15 miles from the fireboat, and Albert thought that the bicycle was the greatest thing. He really enjoyed it and rode it for years. They both were very thankful that he had the bicycle because the city didn't allow firemen any more gasoline than anyone else. That was Albert's transportation back and forth to work

Dolores A. Kelly

Albert playing games at fireman's picnic

for quite some time, and he enjoyed it immensely.

Yet, Albert also suffered his share of bumps and bruises at the fire department, according to a record of his injuries on the job in the fire department. The list started out in 1945 and went up to 1968: thumb injury, back injury, sulfur dioxide injury, fall off a ladder, head injury, another sulfur dioxide injury, another back injury, exposure to something at the Hancock Oil fire on Signal Hill, another back injury, eye injury, two more back injuries (one in 1961 and the other in 1968). In 1961, he fell off an antique fire truck and missed the running board, injuring his back. He had Tinnitus, nerve damage in his ears, so he had a ringing in his ears for about 15 years, the result of all the

Albert's Journey

Albert and Dee Dee on bicycle

loud noise from the sirens, and when he was close to the planes on standby at the airport.

Albert lived with the Tinnitus because it was incurable. He did complain. The pain was not imaginary, and he was approached several times on the job about retiring on a disability, but he said, "Absolutely not." Of course, Albert would not do that. He had such a wonderful job and a contented life that he said, "I just could not apply for a disability to go off of the job." It was something he tolerated because he loved what he did and wanted to continue for as long as he would be permitted. Albert worked 36

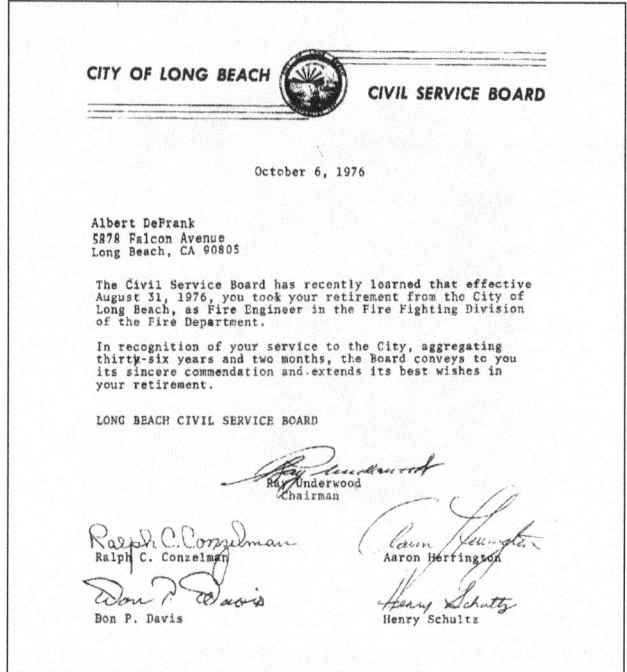

years and two months.

The above citation was from the City of Long Beach. It gave Albert a commendation for his service to the city. The Civil Service Board recognized his service of 36 years and two months offering its best wishes in his retirement. The following two men were Albert's friends and they, too, retired with honors.

Albert's Journey

Kenney Miller

Harold King

Chapter Ten

A Good Life

This book is dedicated to my Uncle Albert. I enjoyed every moment with him and wanted to share my love for him and the family. My residence was in the east with my mother; Uncle Albert's sister, Maria, and I discovered he lived in a place that I wanted to learn as much about it as possible. I had been a teacher of geography and wanted to research what I was teaching. I traveled back and forth across the country many times to enjoy my western family, and, in the process, learned about the United States. It was a constant delight as I saw how people lived in various areas of the country and everything was different from what I knew in the east. The weather was beautiful all year round in California and there were orange groves plus cattle that roamed the hillside. One could see the mountains standing at the ocean and the snow-covered peaks only one hour away by car.

Wading in the ocean while looking at the snowcaps was a time to remember. At that moment I understood why Uncle Albert was fascinated with staying on the west coast for the rest of his life. I can also understand why Uncle Albert married my Aunt Dorothy. She was a kind and loving person, too, and anyone couldn't help but love her wholeheartedly. I don't know what I would have done without her. She was truly an angel and a gift from God in her kindness and gentleness. I only wished that I had spent more time with my western family growing up and through my adult years. However, I have tried to make up for the lost time by keeping in close touch with everyone. In continuing a good life, my intent is to reveal the best things about my uncle and aunt that I can share with everyone.

My Uncle Al was an altruistic and amicable man who never had difficulty making friends. Whenever he entered a room, he immediately felt comfortable meeting everybody, always managing to become that individual's best friend by the end of the conversation. He never met a stranger, Aunt Dorothy said frequently. She told many stories about Uncle Albert helping every person that he ever met, and, of course, she had so many memories of how he assisted and comforted numerous people.

His closest friends were Harold and Carl since before high school and that continued ever after.

Albert's Journey

As noted, his friendship started with Harold on the beach. Yes, challenging him to a fight, and they wrestled and carried on all the rest of their lives. Harold was taller by one inch, but clearly outweighed my uncle. Uncle Albert stayed slim all his life and Harold plumped up and had to go on diets periodically. Aunt Dorothy remembers that no matter what happened the two men stayed together through thick and thin. They treated each other as though they were true brothers.

My aunt never fell short of stories about how Uncle Albert, the fireman, was such a Mr. Nice Guy. He worked 24 hours and was off 24 hours, and no matter where they went there was always someone who needed his help. One day, my Aunt Dorothy and Uncle Albert were looking for a new car to purchase and they were on the west side of Long Beach, which was not a very nice neighborhood at the time. Uncle Albert said, "let's stop and get something to eat," and while they were walking toward a restaurant this dirty old man walked up to him and said, "Would you please give me a quarter for something to eat?" Uncle Albert looked at him and said, "Now look, pop, tell me the truth, do you want a quarter for something to eat or do you want a quarter for a bottle of wine?" The old man said, "I want a bottle of wine." Then Albert took his hand out of his pocket and handed the old fellow a dollar.

Aunt Dorothy stood there annoyed, shaking

her head, and when the old fellow walked away, Aunt Dorothy said, "Al, why did you give him money for wine?" Uncle Albert declared, "You know, if that money will buy him a bottle of wine and he is any more comfortable laying in the gutter when he is sleeping it's worth it." From then on Aunt Dorothy learned to be tight-lipped and never knew how he was figuring things out, but it seemed to her that he was always right. Every place they went there was someone that needed his support. He was a firefighter on duty and a firefighter off duty.

Aunt Dorothy recounted a trip on the way home from Alaska when they were traveling back to Long Beach along the northern coast of California, headed home through the mountains pulling a trailer. They passed a white station wagon and the hood was up. Uncle Albert slowed down and said, "Do you know that's a woman that's in trouble? We're going to have to find a place to park this rig and go back and see if I can help her." They had to continue almost a mile down a mountainside before they could find an area large enough to park the truck and trailer they were hauling. He finally found an area, pulled over to the side, searched for some tools in the truck, and said, "I'm going back to see what the problem is." Aunt Dorothy exclaimed, "I don't want to sit here alone on the side of the road, I'll hike back with you."

Albert's Journey

It was a hot day and a good mile to climb uphill. When they arrived at the car – sure enough – it was a woman alone and she had four children in the car and they were mentally challenged with different limitations. The lady was stranded by the side of the road and acknowledged, "I picked them up at some facility and just wanted to take them out for a Sunday drive and then my car broke down." Uncle Albert discovered it was a broken wire, which he managed to fix and get the car running. Then he suggested to the lady not to be in a hurry when she started to drive. Allow him to get back to his truck and when she drove by he would follow her down the highway to see if she would have any more difficulty with the car. Aunt Dorothy claimed that they followed the lady for several miles. Uncle Albert and Aunt Dorothy had a place where they wanted to stop and he said, "I'm sure she's okay." They both watched her as she accelerated forward. Incidents like this happened all the time.

While traveling on another trip Aunt Dorothy and Uncle Albert were traveling through the desert outside Page, Arizona, journeying down the highway while towing a trailer once again. A young Native American man was running along the highway rolling his tire. He had a flat tire on his car and nobody would stop and give him a ride. He was trying to get back to his car and his family. Uncle Albert said to Aunt Dorothy, "I don't know, I'm going to stop and see what this young man's problem is, and Dot, you take the gun and sit in the back seat and use it only if you have to."

This scared Aunt Dorothy. He stopped and talked with the young man and put the tire in the back of the truck and the man moved into the front seat of the car with Uncle Albert. They chatted for miles; the man was many miles away from his car and his family. When Aunt Dorothy and Uncle Albert arrived at the young man's car Aunt Dorothy recalled seeing his dear old mother sitting on the side of the road in the dirt. He had a wife and two adorable little children. Aunt Dorothy acknowledged that this was a beautiful family and, once again, she worried and thought they were asking for trouble but, as usual, everything turned out just fine.

My uncle and aunt were taking another trip in the Grand Canyon for the Easter Sunrise service. The night before Easter they were about to have a pleasant dinner in the trailer with two steaks, fried potatoes, peppers and onions and Uncle Albert came in the door and said, "Dot, a young man is coming over to have dinner with us." Aunt Dorothy said, "Al, I only have two steaks." He whispered, "Well, just take those steaks and cut them in pieces and put them on a platter, we have enough potatoes and vegetables and that'll be enough."

Aunt Dorothy thought here we go again,

another stranger out of camp. It turned out that he was a very nice young man. He graduated from college and he lived in New York City and told Uncle Albert and Aunt Dorothy his story. He'd purchased a motorcycle and was traveling across the United States and Uncle Albert thought that was fantastic. Of course, Albert reminisced about some of his travels as a young man crisscrossing America. As a result, the young man was their guest for dinner that night, and they had a very pleasant evening. They both thought this was a very special young man. He really enjoyed his dinner that night. He mentioned that he survived for three days on bread and peanut butter. It made my aunt feel very good that they could share a meal with him. The next morning the young man was outside my aunt and uncle's door. He wanted to accompany them to the Easter Sunrise service. Aunt Dorothy said, "The stories just go on and on."

Every time Aunt Dorothy turned around there was somebody to feed, assist, or lend a hand. She said, "This was Mr. Nice Guy." Even though Uncle Albert was tough and rough spoken, he seemed to handle any situation. No one ever annoyed him. He always seemed to take over and be in charge. He had a heart of gold, and definitely Uncle Albert always had to be in the driver's seat no matter where he was.

Dan, his son, recounts a similar story. It took place in 1965 or, perhaps, 1966. Dan had gone to Long Beach City College and was working his first full-time job as a heat treat painter where he did piece work. The company he worked for made drilling bits for petroleum and mining, and Dan would paint the parts, pull them out and spread them on the table. One day, Dan worked a swing shift, which was afternoons, and his dad came into the bedroom as he was getting up for the day. He looked at Dan and said, "You better start sweating boy!" Dan looked at his father and didn't know what he was talking about. Dan said, "What?" Uncle Albert said, "Boy, you better start sweating because some day they will train a monkey and you're going to be out of a job!" Now, that was an example of dad's directness. Dan said, "He was not happy that I had this menial job working in the plant. That was his way of telling me I could do better." Even as he recalls the story, Dan laughs but he always keeps the story close to his heart because he knew then that he could always do better. He eventually owned his own business and has enjoyed a successful career.

Another time while Dan was at Long Beach City College, Uncle Albert gave him some of his wisdom. He assured Dan that he had to look at women with one eye closed. He shortly learned, what he was saying in his own distinctive way, that a man could always find a flaw in a woman or any other aspect of life. That was his way of saying how one copes with life. As he said, "You look with one eye closed."

The other wisdom he passed on to Dan was to handle crap with a shovel. He said, "You can't argue with an idiot." Dan summed up, "My dad was very direct. If I had to be honest, my dad was hard and he expected a lot." Dan always felt as though he couldn't make a mistake.

Another lesson Uncle Albert taught Dan was handling money. Dan was in business for fourteen and one-half years, and was very successful but the reason was because his father always was a simple man. Dan says, "he taught me basics, and drilled them into my head and they were honesty, don't spend money you don't have, take care of the essentials first, and the luxuries come later, if at all."

Albert's advice, consistently direct, was drilled into Dan who is thankful today because he has followed that wisdom. Dan, clearly echoing his father, explained, "That's simple but many people overlook the basics and go for the frills."

Dee Dee, his daughter, was also deeply affected by her father's character. "I was always proud that my father was a fireman. To me that was a very important job. He was capable of protecting life and property. He was always there to help people on or off the job."

Aunt Dorothy said, "Albert was strong, mentally and physically. He was determined and was tough." As a young boy, he bravely sought to find a better life, and his move westward was a matter of survival and determination. It flourished with Aunt Dorothy and succeeded with life in general, his education, and his California family. If Uncle Albert made up his mind to experience something or practice something he managed to do it. Life was a welcome adventure and he lived every day as determined and as energetic as he was when he decided to leave home as a teenager.

As Aunt Dorothy and Uncle Albert started to grow older, they continued to travel frequently even after moving to San Clemente. However, things started to change with Uncle Albert while in San Clemente. The Moldens, Dick and Dot, felt these were the happiest times when Albert and Dorothy lived down the street from them. Dick and Dot both remarked that Albert was a kind, funny man; he had the ability to laugh at himself, was good looking, extremely physically fit, and was great with children. Nevertheless, he could get really hot under the collar, especially arguing politics. Dick and Dot thought it was best to avoid that subject especially because he was so well informed on most of the issues. If Albert told anybody something it was probably true.

Albert's Journey

Dick reminisces, "It was a joy all the time when we were around Al and Dotty. We went for long bike rides every day and we would sit on the porch famished until Dotty would make poor boy sandwiches." As Al would say, "It's lunchmeat with heat." Heat meaning hot peppers.

However, Aunt Dorothy thought when they moved to San Clemente they would never move again, but things happened and Uncle Albert was just not the same. So Aunt Dorothy felt as though she needed to be closer to her son Dan for a little moral support. The house went up for sale and was sold immediately and they moved to Carson City, Nevada. She felt good about the move and still remains there.

Dick recollects when Albert was becoming forgetful. This concerned Aunt Dorothy tremendously. However, if she was closer to Dan things just might be a little better. Dick recalls, "When Al and Dotty moved to Carson City, that was a real sad event." However, Aunt Dorothy and Uncle Albert never lost contact with their "fire family" in Long Beach or their dear friends in San Clemente.

Once in Carson City Uncle Albert would take long walks and Aunt Dorothy continued to worry about him because he would not come home. He started to forget, and was uncertain of his way. While out on one of his walks he was hit by a passing car and was hospitalized. He then became worse, with the forgetfulness, after his recovery from the accident. Uncle Albert needed to be hospitalized anew because he was showing clear signs of Alzheimer's disease. Alzheimer's disease, a brain disorder named for the German doctor Alois Alzheimer, was first described in 1906. Many scientists have learned a great deal about this fatal brain disease. Today, there are about 5.3 million Americans living with this debilitating disease. It destroys brain cells; it is the root of memory loss and difficulty with thinking and behavior. This is relentless enough to affect one's work, hobbies and social life. The disease worsens over time and is fatal, the seventh leading cause of death in the United States. To find more information on this debilitating disease please go to the following website http://www.alz.org/alzheimers_disease_what_is_alzheimers.asp

With the diagnosis, it was impossible for Aunt Dorothy to take care of Uncle Albert physically by herself. Subsequently, she found a facility to assist her and she was able to visit with him every day.

Dee Dee reminisces about visiting her father often. The saddest time she spent with her father was when he was in the nursing home. She remembered, "He looked at me and smiled, but I knew he didn't know who I was."

However, time was not on Uncle Albert's side,

the disease progressed, and he passed away on July 26, 2000.

Dick and Dot Molden remember when he died. "It was the saddest day when Albert passed away." Aunt Dorothy continued to live in Carson City, but explained that she and Uncle Albert had a few good years together in the home they purchased, and she had been blessed for that short time. However, she was warmed by their many years of love together and was fortunate to keep that in her heart. She recently found a sympathy card with a note in it that was written by a retired battalion chief from the city of Long Beach. He wrote:

I am sorry to hear Al passed away. When I was a rookie fireman in the late 1960s I worked a few shifts with him at the Long Beach Airport. He always was a nice man and helped new guys train on the airport crash rigs. The angels will treat him kindly because he was a kind man.

After the death of Uncle Albert, Aunt Dorothy gave Dan his fishing tackle box. Dan was going through the box and came across a small glass bottle. It was Uncle Albert's and it contained some of his mosquito repellent. Now, let's go back to when Dan was five or six years of age. He recalled that Kenny Miller, Uncle Albert's firemen friend, and his wife Pat, Dee Dee and Dan hiked at Lundy Lake. They were going to go fishing and when they arrived Uncle Albert retrieved his tackle box. He recovered his mosquito repellent and started rubbing it on Dan's face. His dad said, "Be a big boy; this is for your own good." When he brought the tackle box home after his dad's passing, he went through it and found the small bottle with a black cap containing mosquito repellent. This comforted Dan and he immediately recaptured his childhood and the time he spent with his dad.

Dan explained what kind of father his dad was and the first word that came to his mind was "direct." He added, "You never had to guess where my dad was coming from because he would let you know. Whether it was a family member or anyone else, when he said 'no' he meant what he said. 'Yes' when he meant yes. There was never a hesitation or a doubt. You always knew what was on his mind. As a child it was hard, but very useful later in life."

Dan feels this philosophy is so basic and missing in so many people. "I would characterize dad as somewhat harsh, but fair. He was the kind of man who was always willing to help others, and that was another valuable lesson that he learned."

As this story closes, it tells the story of an immigrant boy who came to the United States of America. He found that this land was beautiful in every state throughout and he enjoyed life to it fullest. He became a citizen of this fine country and learned many lessons in life that allowed him to see that this, indeed, was the land of the free and the home of the brave.

Epilogue

After many years, Uncle Albert and Grandpop made amends. There were numerous phone calls throughout the years and, eventually, Uncle Emidio and family took Grandpop to visit Uncle Albert in California during the summer of 1958. Uncle Emidio drove 3000 miles across the United States to see his brother. With open arms, Uncle Albert heartily and warmly welcomed his father, brother and family into his home. Everyone was reunited and, during the next 20 years, Uncle Albert and Aunt Dorothy made several trips with the camper across the country to visit his father, brother and sisters. The family was once again united. The anguish of the earlier years was washed away and, with time, Grandpop as well as Uncle Albert mellowed. The family unit was once again complete.

Appendix A

SS Italia 1903-1904

The ship Italia II was 4,806 gross tons, length 400 feet x beam 49.2 feet, one funnel, two masts, single screw and a speed of 14 knots. The accommodations were for 20 first class and 1,400 third class passengers. The ship was built by D. & W. Henderson, Ltd, Glasgow; she was launched for the Anchor Line of Glasgow on December 7, 1903. Her maiden voyage started on February 9, 1904 when she left Genoa for Leghorn, Naples and New York. In May 1918 she made her last Mediterranean - New York voyage, arriving June 6, before being used for three voyages as a North Atlantic troopship. On December 31, 1918 she commenced her first Glasgow - New York sailing and resumed New York - Mediterranean sailings on January 22, 1919. Her last voyage between Trieste, proceeding via Bari, Messina, Palermo and New York started on July 10, 1922 and arrived on July 31 with 15 cabin class passengers and 84 third class passengers; on November 18, 1922 she resumed Glasgow - New York sailings. After one more voyage on this service (comm. January 18, 1923), she was scrapped in June 1923. [North Atlantic Seaway by N. R. P. Bonsor, vol.1, p. 466].

Written with the permission of The Ships List Website
www.theshipslist.com

Appendix B

History of Coatesville, PA

The location of Coatesville is along the Brandywine River in the midst of Chester Valley and mirrors that of many other communities during its development. The first settlement was an Indian village which had grown as a trading center and as a marker for the fur trapping industry. The records indicate land holdings as early as 1714 by William Fleming, a native of Greenock, Scotland. Greenock, lies on the south bank of the Clyde at the Tail of the Bank. The Tail of the Bank was a significant point of embarkation for many travelers, especially emigrants where the River Clyde expands into the Firth of Clyde.

Another early resident, an initial settler in the Coatesville region was a Frenchman Pierre Bizallion. He was an Indian fur trader who settled in the area in the early 18th Century. His accomplishments were recognized with a market place on Oak Street by the Pennsylvania Historic and Museum Commission. He had a very lucrative business with beaver skins. They were in demand in Europe and these skins were shipped back by the thousands where they were tailored into hats and coats.

In addition, he was said to have been an interpreter between William Penn and the Native Americans. William Penn relied on Pierre's dealings with the Indians. His knowledge in the ways of the Indians was invaluable. He acquired roughly 500 acres of land that the Veterans Administration Hospital now sits. He established his own residence at Twelfth

Dolores A. Kelly

Avenue and Olive Streets with his 17 year old bride, the daughter of a Philadelphia trading house owner. She ran away with him and married secretly.

William Fleming, originally from Scotland, is one of the earliest landowners on record and the first white settler. He built a log cabin as a temporary house that was located on the north side of Kersey Street, between Third and Fourth Avenues. He owned about 207 acres of land bordering the Brandywine River. Pierre built a house on the south side of Harmony Street between Fifth and Sixth Avenues for his wife and eight children. One of his sons, Peter, later constructed a mill by the side of the Brandywine and a house that later became part of the Lukens store.

In 1787, Moses, Coates, a prosperous farmer and the area's first postmaster, purchased land that now comprises the center of the town. He purchased the Fleming house from Fleming's son that same year when he was 31. On April 9, 1792 the Pennsylvania General Assembly approved legislation leasing or chartering the Philadelphia and Lancaster Turnpike. The road passed through Coates' property and was the first of its kind in America. The turnpike became a primary main road between Philadelphia and Lancaster.

In 1794, life in the valley changed with the completion of the Philadelphia to Lancaster Turnpike, now it is known as U. S. Route 30. This was America's first turnpike. Moses Coates' son-in-law, Jesse Kersey, a potter by trade and a Quaker missionary by vocation, developed an idea to unfold and expand the area by selling frontage properties on the turnpike. In 1792 the first toll road, the Lancaster Turnpike, was authorized and in 1794 life in the valley changed with the completion of the Turnpike in 1795. The tollgate was positioned within the Coatesville city limits. This was a popular rest stop located half way between Lancaster and Philadelphia.

Further south, Isaac Pennock was formulating plans for his Federal Slitting Mill, later known as Rokeby. In 1793 it was operating and furnished the needed iron products for the growing region. A partnership was formed between Jesse Kersey and the ironmaster Isaac Pennock. In 1810 they purchased 110.5 acres of Coates' farm that lay along both sides of the Brandywine River. The farm's sawmill was converted to an ironworks and named Brandywine Iron Works and Nail Factory. This was the forerunner of Lukens Steel, Inc.

In 1812 Moses Coates became the area's first postmaster. He had two marriages that produced a dozen children. Jesse was his youngest son and became the village doctor. His daughter Elizabeth married Jesse Kersey. He was a Quaker missionary and bought a farm in East Caln Township. He has been described as Coatesville's first real estate agent. From his father-in-law he purchased 13 acres east of First Avenue. Then he divided the property into lots for building along Harmony and Kersey Streets, and selected the name Coates Villa in honor of his father-in-law.

The village of Coates Villa became modernized with the name of Coatesville, and the oldest and largest continuously operating steel mill (producers of plate steel) in America were launched together. In 1813 Charles Lukens, MD married Isaac Pennock's daughter

Dolores A. Kelly

Rebecca. When her husband passed away in 1825 Rebecca took over the operations of the mill, purchasing it from her mother and shepherding it through turmoil and market panic into a prosperous mill.

In 1834 a major event in the region was the construction of the Philadelphia and Columbia Railroad where a station was established on the west side of the Brandywine. Due to its location, at the halfway point between the two terminals, it was designated as "Midway," and the village that quickly formed around the terminal took the same name. The village of Coatesville and the village of Midway joined to form the Borough of Coatesville in 1867.

The Pennsylvania Railroad along with its precursor the Philadelphia and Columbia had served Midway for 30 years. Many stores were launched connecting First and Third Avenue on the Lancaster Turnpike; in addition, new homes were built. Coatesville continued to operate as a borough until 1915, when the citizens voted for it to become the first and only city in Chester County.

In 1912 President Theodore Roosevelt came to the city, and Buffalo Bill Cody and his Wild West Show called the city their winter home during the late 19th Century.

Coatesville was the fastest growing community of many diverse cultures. The town's mills attracted immigrants with job offers and many southern and central European immigrants fled to the area. The housing accommodations could not keep up with the flood of new immigrants. Newspapers ignored the foreigners in their columns. However, on October 2, 1909, the Coatesville Record, the town's newspaper

Albert's Journey

printed a notable story criticizing the manner in which the police treated the town's new residents. Most of the immigrants spoke little English, had no attorney to defend themselves or anyone to advise them. They paid their fines and thought this was the American way. It was not. It was questioned why men were dragged away from their homes and thrown into jail; the paper suggested an investigation should be made.

The men were considered excellent unskilled workmen at low wages. Merchants had no complaints because they brought business to their stores. They generally paid cash and could be trusted and dependable upon settling their accounts.

During the 1920s Chester County had about 115,000 residents. This was the beginning of prohibition, January 17, 1920 at 12:01 am. Many Chester County women celebrated the arrival of "dry weather" by participating in special events to mark the occasion (Woodward, 2002, p. 108).

Band concerts were the form of entertainment and a favorite during the twenties. Sports events gained popularity during the 1920s. In 1927 the Coatesville Record gave extensive coverage on the "fight of the century" between Tunney and Dempsey. The Record also placed a power speaker outside its office so fans could listen to the ring announcer in Chicago as the ten round match unfolded.

Columbus Day 1928 was now a legal holiday in all the states, except 13. It became a federal holiday nine years later in 1937. This served to perpetuate the memory, discovery and exploration that enlarged our earth. The Sons of Italy in America sponsored a celebration in honor of Columbus. The opening ceremonies were held in front of City Hall. A band known as Pizza's Band arrived from Philadelphia for the event. They played the Star Spangled Banner and the Italian Royal March in which three bombs exploded: the first sent an American flag up attached to a parachute, the second released an Italian flag in the same manner and the third contained a picture of Columbus and a ship. The band marched through the city and spent hours giving concerts in various locations. The festivities concluded when the band reached Our Lady of the Rosary Church and a magnificent display of fireworks concluded the celebration.

In baseball, 1929 was an excellent year. Connie Mack's Athletics became world champions after the A's won their second straight World Series game against the Chicago Cubs.

The stock market crashed in 1929. This made for the worst panic in Wall Street's history. Coatesville in the 1930s were a time of hardship and hunger, unemployment and the stagnation of business. There were many farms that were foreclosed and banks that failed. Optimism was at an all time low.

On August 1, 1934 Amelia Earhart was observed dining at the Coach and Four Inn, the community's premier eating establishment. Upon leaving the restaurant a reporter from the *Record* was waiting to interview her. She related to him she was returning to New York from a holiday in Wyoming. The journalist found "Lady Lindy" to be gracious and accommodating. She told the journalist, "This looks like a fine little city, and this is the best meal we've had since leaving Wyoming." She was met by

Albert's Journey

the president of the fire company, Frank E. Soule and Clarence W. McConnell, Councilman with a bouquet of flowers and invited to visit the Washington Hose Company. She accepted the invitation amiably and spoke at the firehouse with a promise to return. However, she never returned to Coatesville. The aviator vanished after taking off from a New Guinea airstrip on one of the final legs of her journey around the world (Woodward, 2002, p. 134).

Reprinted with permission from Coatesville by Bruce Edward Mowday. Available from the publisher online at www.arcadiapublishing.com or by calling 888-313-2665.

Written with the permission of Admin@coatesville.org
www.coatesville.org/visitors/history.asp

Coatesville Revisited by Wayne C. Woodward
W. C. Woodward (personal communication, October 27, 2010) discussed the history of Coatesville.

Dolores A. Kelly

Appendix C

History of the Coatesville Train Station

The oldest existing station along the Pennsylvania Railroad's Main Line is the Coatesville train station located at Third Avenue and Fleetwood Streets. This two story Italianate style station was built in 1865. The facility has an enclosed shelter on a platform with period windows and arcaded passageways. The station building has been abandoned for well over 20 years and was included in the Preserving Pennsylvania's 2003 "Pennsylvania at Risk" report as one of the states's most endangered historic properties.

Since that time, city and regional officials have pushed forward planning for a major redevelopment of the station complex as well as the surrounding neighborhood and town, hoping to capitalize on recent growth in the area as well as generate new commercial, residential and transit expansion.

In 2003, the city of Coatesville received funding from the Knight Fellowship Program in Community Building to look at opportunities to revitalize the station's neighborhood along the principles of Smart Growth and New Urbanism. The goal was to create a program to "restore the station as the gateway to the historic, commercial and professional center of Coatesville." Citing changing demographics including an increase in population as justification for the project's timeliness, the report proposed the development of a new multi-modal interchange directly adjacent to the train station, which would be

Albert's Journey

fully accessible and include a new bus depot, a taxi stop, cycle parking and lockers, a travel information center and a tourist information kiosk.

An expanded station, proposed retail storefronts and a new parking garage could potentially turn the area into a transit and commercial focal point. However, the timeline and costs of the project are significant. Currently, the area's only public commuter service is Krapf's Transit, a bus line that picks up a quarter-mile from the train station and connects with SEPTA.

Coatesville's history, in some ways, mirrors that of its train station. The economy of Coatesville used to be centered mostly on steel production, specifically as the home of Lukens Steel, which has since gone through several acquisitions to become the ArcelorMittal Steel Company. With America's general transition from a manufacturing economy to a service economy, Coatesville saw economic declines generally in line with those experienced by others and became economically distressed. The train station closed, some business moved away from the city and the crime rates rose.

Recently, however, the city and the region have been undergoing redevelopment as Chester County has become the beneficiary of increasing demands for residential, recreational and retail facilities. Coatesville's location near Philadelphia as well as its relatively low-cost and available property has made it a prime competitor for this expanding market.

As Coatesville and Chester County continue to grow and transform, renovation of the abandoned train station seems on the horizon, a fitting capstone

Dolores A. Kelly

to the area's resurrection. However, Amtrak does not provide ticketing or baggage services at this facility, nevertheless, Coatesville is served by an average of eight trains a day. Amtrak's Keystone Service is financed in part through funds made available by the Commonwealth of Pennsylvania Department of Transportation.

Written with the permission of Amtrak.com on behalf of
Great American Stations
www.GreatAmericanStations.com

Appendix D

Long Beach, CA

The Spanish explorer Juan Rodríguez Cabrillo and his crew sailed in the ships San Salvador, Victoria, and San Miguel, landed upon the shores of what would ultimately become Long Beach, California 50 years after Columbus discovered America. He named the area "Bahia de los Fumos" – which translates to "Bay of Smokes." Cabrillo witnessed clouds of smoke rising from the top of what we know today as Signal Hill. The Native American Indians (Tongva) who occupied the region used smoke signals as a form of communication to those living on Santa Catalina Island (legend has it that Cabrillo was buried there after dying from a fall on January 3, 1543).

Although Cabrillo's journey to Alta California took place in 1542, Spain was not serious in gaining power of the discovered coastal regions for another 200 years. Baja was their northwest boundary and where efforts to settle the land and convert the native tribes to Christianity and the European way of life were unproductive.

Traveling north from Baja was treacherous and proved complex. Ocean currents and coastal winds were hostile and the Spanish captains could not find protected harbors for their crafts. Spain did not make a concerted effort to undertake this journey and colonize Alta California until after the Seven Years War (1756-1763) when European alliances along with their colonial empires were realigned.

In 1769, Spain set forth land and sea expeditions

Dolores A. Kelly

to Alta California and established presidios (forts), missions, and pueblos (towns). Land grants were given to create ranchos with the point of drawing settlers and encouraging development. In 1784, the largest Spanish land grant of 300,000 acres was awarded to Manual Nieto. A land dispute however, whittled the amount of land to almost half. Nieto's acreage extended from the hills north of Whittier to the Pacific Ocean and from San Gabriel River (Los Angeles River) to the Santa Ana River. "Rancho Los Nietos" was the first modern identity for Long Beach. As time passed, the descendants divided the land and ultimately ended up with two ranchos – Los Cerritos and Los Alamitos.

After the collapse of the Spanish empire in 1821, Mexico (which was one of their occupied territories) affirmed its independence and claimed California. However, Californians had been autonomous for so long that they simply never acknowledged nor had reverence for the governors sent from Mexico. Those with power were descendants of the Spanish soldiers who were now owners of large and permanent rancho land grants.

Manuel Nieto's daughter, Manuela Cota inherited Rancho Los Cerritos – "Ranch of the Little Hills." After she passed away, the Rancho was sold by her heirs in 1843 to John Temple from Massachusetts. In 1844, Temple built a two-story Monterey-style adobe which served as his headquarters for his large-scale cattle operation. In 1866, Rancho Los Cerritos was sold to Lewellyn Bixby of Flint, Bixby & Company.

This Adobe is a vital exhibit of Spanish, Mexican and American California history which depicts

Albert's Journey

the transition of Southern California's ranching beginnings to a modern and urban society. Today it is a National, State and Long Beach Historic Landmark as well as a public museum. Rancho Los Alamitos – "The Little Cottonwoods" or "Poplars" was bought in 1844 by Massachusetts native and Yankee merchant "Don" Abel Stearns for use as a summer home. Stearns resided in Los Angeles with his wife Arcadia who was from the wealthy Bandini family. His father-in-law, Juan Bandini was an early leader and one of the most well-known businessmen in Southern California during his time. Bandini's fortune was made through farming, stock raising and merchandising. He was also one of the leading rancho owners in Mexican California.

Stearns was one of the largest landowners in Southern California, a successful merchant with a profitable business, cattle rancher, politician, surveyor and one of the richest, well-respected and key citizens in the town. Unfortunately, the worst drought in Southern California which followed the series of severe flooding during the winter of 1861 and 1862 brought misfortune to Stearns. Cattle starved and died, there was an epidemic of smallpox and property values plummeted in 'cow counties.'

The drought was financially destructive for Stearns. He lost control of Los Alamitos, his favorite ranch. Stearns took a mortgage against the ranch from Michael Reese and the property ended up in foreclosure. Reese then leased the land in 1878 to Lewellyn Bixby's cousin John Bixby.

J. Bixby & Company, together with John Bixby and I. W. Hellman, purchased Rancho Los Alamitos

Dolores A. Kelly

in 1881 and for the next 90 years, the Bixby family which was one of the largest landowners of the 20th Century in Los Angeles area, occupied Los Alamitos. It would later be referred to as the "Bixby Ranch."

In 1968, the city of Long Beach was granted the furnished ranch house, six barns and gardens by the surviving trustees of the Bixby Home Property Trust so that they could maintain and develop it as a regional historic and educational facility.

In 1881, real estate developer William Erwin Willmore entered into a lease provided by Jotham Bixby. The lease had an option to buy 4000 acres which was to be developed into a city and agricultural community along the coast. The township of Willmore City was established in 1882 and was promoted throughout the United States. Unfortunately, the response was dismal and two years later, there were only about a dozen homes.

In 1884, the Long Beach Land & Water company bought out Willmore's lease option and the city was renamed Long Beach. Willmore's exclusive design and layout of the city, however, was not discarded and the extra wide streets and Lincoln Park are still in existence today. The city of Long Beach was incorporated in July of 1887.

The few settlers in Long Beach choose to remain in the small town. However, by 1887 and 1888, Long Beach experienced a great boom. Railroad service was provided by Southern Pacific and the Santa Fe Railway that brought in hordes of visitors to Long Beach, now considered an established seaside resort. The real estate market exploded and new developments throughout the city were well underway.

Albert's Journey

Over the years as the transit system continued to become more efficient, growth remained steady and Long Beach flourished. Not only was the city considered a resort, but by the early 1900s, it was also known as a commercial center.

During the years between 1902 and 1910, Long Beach was the fastest growing city in the United States. In 1897, the population was 1500 and within an area of three square miles. In 1914, the population increased to 48,000, in 1954 it was 285,000 and today a population of almost half a million is living within a 50 square mile area.

In 1911, the Port of Long Beach was officially in business. It has grown from 800 acres of mudflats at the mouth of the Los Angeles River to over 3,200 acres today. The Port of Long Beach is the second busiest in the United States, the twelfth busiest container cargo port in the world and it is a premier gateway for trade between the United States and Asia.

Oil was discovered in Signal Hill in 1921 after several unsuccessful drilling attempts and serious doubt it even existed in this location. As a result, many became rich and Long Beach thrived. Signal Hill field, which later became known as Long Beach field became the biggest producer in Southern California and is recognized as producing more oil per acre than anywhere else in the world.

On March 10, 1933, Long Beach experienced an earthquake with an estimated magnitude of 6.25 on the Richter scale. Loss of life totaled 120 and damage was widespread throughout Southern California. Among the many buildings severely damaged or destroyed were schools in or near Long Beach.

Specifically because of these structural failures of unreinforced masonry schools, that the Field Act, which mandates all school buildings, must be earthquake-resistant was passed. Downtown Long Beach also suffered widespread damage and was rebuilt in Art Deco style.

In 1941, The U.S. Naval base was constructed in the Long Beach Harbor.

Howard Hughes' famous H-4 Hercules, nicknamed Spruce Goose took off over the Long Beach Harbor in 1947 and made its first and only flight. It flew for only one minute and traveled one mile at an altitude of 70 feet. Hughes contributed $7 million of his own money and an additional $18 million in government funds to construct this massive cargo plane designed to transport up to 750 armed troops or two 30-ton tanks during WWII. Due to complications, the aircraft was not complete until after the war was over. The Spruce Goose was the world's largest airplane at the time. It continues to hold the record as the largest flying boat, largest wingspan, tallest airplane and the largest aircraft ever made from wood.

In 1983, Hughes' massive creation was exhibited in the world's largest geodesic dome adjacent to the Queen Mary. However, in 1993, the Spruce Goose was moved to Evergreen Aviation in McMinnville, Oregon where it is on display.

In 1949, California State University Long Beach was founded. Originally named Los Angeles-Orange County State College, it offered 25 courses which were taught in two apartment buildings. One year later, Long Beach citizens voted collectively to acquire 320 acres for a permanent campus at a cost of one million dollars.

It is believed a portion of the campus is located on the site of the ancient Tongva village and burial site recognized as Puvunga which is an area listed on the National Register of Historic Places. There were disagreements over the land when the university attempted to construct a strip mall. A lawsuit was filed by the Tongva people and a protest ensued. To date, this last undeveloped portion of the campus remains untouched by builders.

California State University Long Beach is also known as Cal State Long Beach, Long Beach State, LBSU, CSULB or simply The Beach. It is the second largest campus in the California State University system and has impressive reviews in these following publications: U.S. News and World Report's America's Best Colleges Guide, The Princeton Review and America's Best Value Colleges.

One of Long Beach's most famous residents, the Queen Mary, is permanently docked in the Long Beach Harbor. The Queen Mary's journey began in 1936 when it made its maiden voyage from Southampton, England to Cherbourg, France. The next day the Queen Mary continued its journey across the North Atlantic Ocean to Pier 90 in New York. On December 11, 1967, the Queen Mary was removed from British registry after completing 1,001 crossings of the Atlantic and officially turned over to the City of Long Beach. This magnificent luxury cruise liner is listed on the National Register of Historic Places and docked in the Long Beach Harbor. It is a major tourist attraction, convention center and a first-class hotel.

Dolores A. Kelly

In the mid-seventies, the control of downtown Long Beach redevelopment was turned over to the city by the State Coastal Commission and a multi-billion dollar redevelopment plan continued through 2000. Many exciting changes were taking place. The first Long Beach Grand Prix was held in 1977 through the streets of downtown. The winner, Mario Andretti, became the first American to win a U.S. Grand Prix. The race was a huge success and made news in Sports Illustrated and the New York Times as well as coverage in the local and national media. This exciting event, now called the Toyota Grand Prix of Long Beach continues today and is held every spring.

The Long Beach Convention Center opened in 1978, four Olympic events were held during the 1984 Los Angeles Olympics and Southern California's largest aquarium and the nation's fifth largest, The Aquarium of the Pacific opened in 1998. Long Beach is home to the Congressional Cup, Transpac and Olympic trial races. New retail development included Shoreline Village, The Pike and City Place.

Long Beach is recognized as a thriving waterfront destination for tourists. This vibrant, world-class city features numerous attractions, fabulous shopping districts, a beautiful Art Deco downtown, historic buildings, recreational activities, festivals, Broadway shows, great restaurants and terrific waterfront dining.

Written with the permission of longbeach.com
http://www.longbeach.com/history.html

Appendix E

Long Beach Polytechnic High School

In 1895 Long Beach Polytechnic High School, more commonly known as Poly, was founded. It is located at 1600 Atlantic Avenue, Long Beach, California. This is the flagship school for the Long Beach Unified School District. Polytechnic has long been distinguished in athletics and academics. The motto of the school is "Home of Scholars & Champions' and 'Enter to Learn, Go Forth to Serve." Their mascot is the Jackrabbit and the yearbook is known as Caerulea.

Polytechnic High School is the flagship high school of the Long Beach Unified School District. It is a large urban high school with just over 5,000 students.

Classes began in 1895 at the Methodist Tabernacle Chapel in the fall. The school was located on the NE corner of Third Street and Locust Avenues. The principal was Walter S. Bailey and the teacher was Hattie Mason who taught English, Math, History, Latin, Greek and German to 28 students.

On June 18, 1897 the first and only graduate was Ernest Shaul. Later classes relocated to Chautauqua Hall at Fourth Street and Pine Avenue as work commences on the new Long Beach High School at Eight Street at American Avenue that is now Long Beach Boulevard.

In 1898 the Long Beach High School was dedicated on May 20. The building style was mission with a red tile roof. There were four classrooms and an assembly hall.

The Long Beach High School Athletic Association

was formed in 1899. A semi pro baseball team donated uniforms to the high school and the result of this the school colors were changed from red and white to match the uniforms to green and gold.

Courtney A. Teel graduated in 1902 as the first student to go through every grade in the Long Beach school.

In 1903 the first Long Beach High School year book, "Caerulea" was published, and in 1904 football and basketball came to Poly.

The first student government was formed in 1906.

The year 1907 was significant. David "Daddy" Brucham became principal. He held that title until 1941. In addition, the girl's basketball team won the first three sequential state championships.

A debate began in 1909 on a site for a new Polytechnic High School with a curriculum designed after the Los Angeles schools.

In 1910 the corner of 16th Street and Atlantic Avenue was chosen as the school's new and larger permanent site.

Long Beach Polytechnic High School opened in 1911 with 31 teachers and 850 students. That same year California's first PTA was formed.

In 1914 the California Interscholastic Federation was formed and a girl's athletic league.

JROTC was introduced in 1917. During the years 1917-1918 an influenza epidemic and World War I intruded school life and sports. The name "Jackrabbits" was inspired by the many rabbits that roamed the athletic field. The track team decided to have their mascot as the "Jackrabbits." December

Albert's Journey

27 the old high school burned and served well as an elementary school. In World War I there were 22 students that gave their lives.

On January 18, 1924 the David Burcham Field, the Poly Athletic Field was dedicated.

The school year 1924-1925 the school reached an enrollment of 3,750 students. During the 1920s Polytechnic was the largest school west of the Mississippi River.

Woodrow Wilson High opened in eastern Long Beach in 1925 and quickly became the chief rival of Poly High.

Five CIF titles were captured in 1929. They were football, basketball, cross country, swimming and water polo.

A new auditorium was constructed in 1931 at a cost of $200,000.

March 10, 1933 a 6.3 earthquake hit the area and the school's towering dome at the school entrance collapsed. Many buildings were ruined and the science building was burned to the ground. The following week school reopened in 47 tents on Burcham Field. This was known as "Tent City." This remained for three years. Bricks from the high school were sold as souvenirs after the earthquake. The proceeds paid for a memorial flagpole that now stands in the center of the campus.

A new science building was constructed in 1935 and the auditorium was remodeled. The architect Hugh Davies authors the school motto "Enter to Learn, Go Forth to Serve." A new administration building opened in 1936 and 1,006 students graduated in 1937. This was the first class to graduate over 1,000 students.

Dolores A. Kelly

During the years of 1941 to 1944 there were several occurrences. Principal "Daddy" Burcham retired and the United Stated entered into World War II. Victory Gardens were grown by the Poly students as well as joined bond and scrap drives. A quantity of 4,000 Poly students and staff enlisted to fight the war. There were 77 that died. A number of the students fought before they graduated and many came back to finish their studies and receive their diplomas; however, many students missed out on senior year activities because of the war. Several male teachers were drafted into service and they were replaced by female teachers.

In 1945 Poly celebrated its 50th anniversary. The Douglas Aircraft Company built "The Spirit of Poly," a bomber plane that was financed with war bonds sold by the students. The plane flew over the campus that reinforced the spirit and patriotism of the student body.

Written with the permission Poly Class of '58
reunion committee
http://lbpoly58.com/id6.html

References

Abruzzo World Club 2000. (2009, May 29). Province of Teramo. Retrieved May 29, 2009, from http://www.abruzzo2000.com/abruzzo/teramo/index.html

Author. (2010). Visual and textual chronology for prosaic messages (Picture). Retrieved October 15, 2010, from http://www.usm.maine.edu/~amoroso/courses/chron.html

Barzini, L. (1965). *The Italians.* New York: Atheneum

Bonsor, N.R.P. (1975). *North atlantic seaway.* (Rev. 2nd ed. p. 466). New York: Arco Publishing Company, Inc.

Caerulea Students. (1934). *The new polytechnic Caerulea year Book 1934.* Vol. 31. May 14, 2008

Castello Cities Internet Network, Inc. (2010). *The history of Long Beach.* Retrieved October 9, 2010, from http://www.longbeach.com/history.html

Coatesville, Pennsylvania. (2010, October 24). In *Wikipedia, The Free Encyclopedia*. Retrieved 19:55, October 26, 2010, from http://en.wikipedia.org/w/index.php?title=Coatesville,_Pennsylvania&oldid=392688615

D'Onofrio Flocco, C. (1994). *The book of Abruzzo: Back to our roots*. Pierre Congress srl: Pescara, Italia

Duggan, C. (1994). *A concise history of Italy*. Cambridge: University Press

Engle, H.M. (1933). Long Beach, California, (Pictures) *Earthquake March 10, 1933*. Retrieved April 10, 2009, from U. S. Geological Survey. (2007). USGS Science for a changing world. U.S. Department of the Interior, U.S. Geological Survey, Reston, VA, USA http://libraryphoto.cr.usgs.gov/cgi-bin/search.cgi?search_mode=exact&selection=Long+Beach%2C+California%2C+Earthquake+March+10%2C+1933%7CLong+Beach%7CEarthquake%7C1933

History of Coatesville. (n. d.). Retrieved October 9, 2010, from http://www.coatesville.org/visitors/history.asp

Italy-Weather and Maps. (2009, May 29). Abruzzo Region (Map). Retrieved May 29, 2009, from http://www.worldatlas.com

Long Beach Polytechnic High School. (2010, October 19). In *Wikipedia, The Free Encyclopedia*. Retrieved 14:55, October 26, 2010, from http://en.wikipedia.org/w/index.php?title=Long_Beach_Polytechnic_High_School&oldid=391594372

Macalwane, S. J. James B. (1933). (Pictures). Lynwood Tank. Steinbrugge Collection, NISEE/PEER and The University of California, Berkeley. Retrieved September 01, 2010, from http://www.eas.slu.edu/Earthquake_Center/1933LBeq/001.html

Mowday, B. E. (2003). *Images of America: Coatesville*. Charleston, SC: Arcadia Publishing

Poly Class of '58 Reunion Committee. (2010). Poly's historical timeline. Retrieved October 26, 21010, from http://lbpoly58.com/id6.html

Revitalizing America's Train Stations. (n. d.). Retrieved October 13, 2010, from http://www.GreatAmericanStations.com/Stations/COT/Station_view

Smith, D. M. (1959). *Italy*. Ann Arbor: The University of Michigan Press.

Sforza, C. (1949). *Italy and the Italians*. New York: E. P. Dutton & Company, Inc.

Slutske, R. V. (2007). The pike celebrates past, present and future. *Destinations* 2007, 30-31.

Swiggum, S. & Kohli, M. (n.d.). *The ship's list* (Fact sheet). Retrieved from http://www.theshipslist.com/ships/descriptions/

Trevelyan, J. P. (1920). *A short history of the Italian people*. New York: Pitman Publishing Corporation.

U. S. Geological Survey. (2006, April 20). USGS Science for a changing world. U.S. Department of the Interior, .S. Geological Survey, Reston, VA, USA (Pictures). Retrieved June 3, 2009, from http://libraryphoto.cr.usgs.gov/cgi-bin/search.cgi?search_mode=exact&selection=Long+Beach%2C+California%2C+Earthquake+March+10%2C+1933%7CLong+Beach%7CEarthquake%7C1933

U. S. Geological Survey. (2006, April 20). USGS Photographic Library (Engle Pictures). Retrieved June 3, 2009, from U. S. Geological Survey Photographic Library at http://libraryphoto.cr.usgs.gov/cgi-bin/search.cgi?search_mode=exact&selection=Long+Beach%2C+California%2C+Earthquake+March+10%2C+1933%7CLong+Beach%7CEarthquake%7C1933

What is Alzheimer's? (2010, September 10). Alzheimer's Association. Retrieved September 10,2010, from http://www.alz.org/alzheimers_disease_what_is_alzheimers.asp

Woodward, W. C. (2002). *Coatesville revisited*. (pp. 1-135). Wagontown, PA: Herb Leslie Printing.

www.ingramcontent.com/pod-product-compliance
Lightning Source LLC
Chambersburg PA
CBHW061642040426
42446CB00010B/1538